Meaning &
Interpretation

Meaning & Interpretation

Wittgenstein, Henry James, and Literary Knowledge

G. L. HAGBERG

Cornell University Press

Ithaca and London

Open access edition funded by the National Endowment for the Humanities/ Andrew W. Mellon Foundation Humanities Open Book Program.

Copyright © 1994 by Cornell University

All rights reserved. Except for brief quotations in a review, this book, or parts thereof, must not be reproduced in any form without permission in writing from the publisher. For information, address Cornell University Press, Sage House, 512 East State Street, Ithaca, New York 14850, or visit our website at cornellpress.cornell.edu.

First published 1994 by Cornell University Press

Library of Congress Cataloging-in-Publication Data

Hagberg, Garry, 1952–
   Meaning and interpretation : Wittgenstein, Henry James, and literary knowledge / G.L. Hagberg.
     p. cm.
   Includes bibliographical references (p.) and index.
   ISBN-13: 978-0-8014-2926-2 (cloth) — ISBN-13: 978-1-5017-2696-5 (pbk.)
   1. James, Henry, 1843–1916—Criticism and interpretation. 2. Fiction—History and criticism—Theory, etc. 3. Wittgenstein, Ludwig, 1889–1951. 4. Knowledge, Theory of, in literature. 5. Meaning (Philosophy) in literature. I. Title.
2124.H34   1994
121'.68'092—dc20   93-36146

An open access (OA) ebook edition of this title is available under the following Creative Commons license: Attribution-NonCommercial-NoDerivatives 4.0 International (CC BY-NC-ND 4.0): https://creativecommons.org/licenses/by-nc-nd/4.0/. For more information about Cornell University Press's OA program or to download our OA titles, visit cornellopen.org.

To the memory of my father

Contents

	Acknowledgments	ix
	Introduction	1
1	Language-Games and Artistic Styles	9
	The Concept of a Language-Game *10*	
	Linguistic and Artistic Microcosms *17*	
	Style, Coherence, and Artistic Limits *24*	
2	Forms of Life and Artistic Practices	45
	The Concept of a Form of Life *46*	
	Gesture, Ritual, and Artistic "Spirit" *59*	
	Meaning and Artistic Uses *69*	
3	Circumstances of Significance	84
	"The Author of Beltraffio" *84*	
	Descriptions In Situ *89*	
	Tone and Gestural Expression *95*	

4   Aspects of Interpretation   104
      "The Lesson of the Master" *105*
      Against Reductionism *129*
      "The Figure in the Carpet" *139*

5   Interpretation and Philosophical Method   149
      "The Tree of Knowledge" *151*
      Epistemological Fiction *157*
      Literary Interpretation and Philosophical
         Investigation *169*

   Index   179

∽ Acknowledgments

I initially drafted much of what follows at Cambridge University, where I presented parts of the work in progress to various seminars and meetings. I thank everyone with whom I discussed this project as it developed, especially John MacKinnon, Hugh Mellor, Alex Neill, Robert Stern, and George Watson. I also thank Colin Lyas and Michael Tanner, whose detailed commentary on an earlier draft sharpened the focus of the entire project. Most of all, I thank Renford Bambrough, who allowed me to present sections of this book to his seminars and read and commented extensively on each part as it developed as well as on the entire manuscript. I cannot overstate the philosophical benefit I derived from those many meetings and conversations, and the careful reader will see throughout the extent to which my work refers to his.

I also thank a great many people and institutions on this side of the Atlantic, including, at the Pennsylvania State University at Harrisburg, William Mahar, head of the Humanities Division, and Howard Sachs, dean for Research and Graduate Studies (both of whom put many resources at my disposal); the Research Initiation Grant Program and the Institute for the Arts and Humanistic Studies, both of which supported the work with fellowships; and a few individuals who stand out from a larger, very supportive crowd: Donald Wolff, Troy Thomas, and, most particularly, Louise Hoffman. I presented sections of the work in progress to meetings of the American Society for Aesthetics and to the International Association for Philosophy and Literature, and I am also grateful for the support and fully comprehending commentary of Laurent Stern, Lydia Goehr, and Henry Alexander, whom I thank especially for his enduring encouragement. From Richard Eldridge I received not only one but two extremely astute, constructive, and very finely detailed readings of earlier versions, both of which proved enormously helpful. I thank as well the National Endowment for the Humanities for supporting my work in Cambridge and my participation in the Institute for Theory and Interpretation in the Visual Arts at Hobart and William Smith Colleges in 1987. Of the many people to whom I am indebted from that utopian experience I must particularly mention Michael Podro and Annabel Wharton for sustained conversation on a range of aesthetic issues. Also, my good friends Allen Cox, Edward Wight, and the late Howard Roberts helped with many conversations in their areas of expertise (painting, musicology, and music performance respectively). I also acknowledge my debt to Bard College not only for providing a superb context for aesthetic scholarship but also for supporting further work in Cambridge with an Asher B. Edelman fellowship, and my debt to my colleagues in philosophy, William Griffith and Daniel Berthold-Bond, whose philosophical engagement I have found consistently inspiring.

Chapter 5 was previously published in slightly different form in *Philosophy and Literature* 13 (April 1989): 75–95, edited by Denis Dutton; I thank the Johns Hopkins University Press for permission to incorporate it here and the editor for publishing the piece initially. The remainder of the work is published here for the first time. Last, I am indebted to Roger Haydon of Cornell University Press, who has given this project much in addition to the patient encouragement it needed, and to Andrew Lewis, whose very fine copy-editing proved extremely helpful at the final stages.

All of the above-mentioned people have made this a better work than it would have been without them (although it does not follow from this fact that any of them would agree with what I've written); indeed, given the quantity and quality of the support this work has enjoyed, it is very much more than a *pro forma* move in a narrowly circumscribed language-game to say that with regard to any remaining flaws, I am entirely on my own. Carol Brener, Kathleen Elliot, René Horley, Kathleen Jacob, Marie Ratchford, and Janice Russ very kindly and patiently prepared the manuscripts, and to them I remain extremely grateful.

GARRY HAGBERG

Annandale-on-Hudson, New York

Meaning & Interpretation

~ Introduction

Given the importance of the concept of meaning to discussions of the arts and literature, and given the importance of the philosophy of Ludwig Wittgenstein to our understanding of that concept, it seems somewhat curious that scholars in aesthetics and literary theory have made no more use of Wittgenstein's potentially illuminating work than they have. In this book I attempt to do exactly that, in the hope of shedding some light on the relations between linguistic and artistic meaning, between understanding persons and understanding works of art, and between literary interpretation and philosophical analysis. I hope to achieve results more affirmative or positive in nature than those usually associated with philosophy and criticism of a broadly Wittgensteinian sort. Indeed, the Wittgensteinian tradition has often been construed as little more than a project of confusion-removal, which closes and narrows rather than opens and expands explanatory directions and possibilities. I have much more to say about the more affirmative and illuminating aspects of the Wittgensteinian tradition, and about the dubiousness of the distinction between constructive and critical methodological categories. At present, however, a few words are in order about how Wittgenstein's work has been received by those working within the disciplinary boundaries of aesthetics and literary criticism.

Wittgenstein's idea of family resemblance, as a contribution to the problem of universals, has been applied to the problem of definition in the arts, and this application has profoundly changed the expectations within aesthetics of how discussions of definition in the arts could proceed.[1] Wittgenstein's work on aspect perception and the nature of imaginative seeing has also been applied to the study of the interrelations between the perceiver and the perceived, and this work has profoundly changed expectations within aesthetics of how discussions of those problems would proceed.[2] And that seems to be the extent of the acknowledged significance of Wittgenstein's philosophy for aesthetic theory; the not-unreasonable consensus—given the limited range of Wittgenstein's work that has been examined—is that this integration of Wittgenstein's influence has been completed and that the time has come to return to the fundamental task of theory construction.[3] As I attempt to

---

1. See, for example, Morris Weitz, "The Role of Theory in Aesthetics," *Journal of Aesthetics and Art Criticism* 15 (Fall 1957), and "Wittgenstein's Aesthetics," in *Language and Aesthetics*, ed. B. R. Tilghman (Lawrence: University of Kansas Press, 1973).

2. See, for example, Virgil Aldrich, *Philosophy of Art* (Englewood Cliffs, N.J.: Prentice-Hall, 1963); Roger Scruton, *Art and Imagination* (London: Methuen, 1974); and John Casey, *The Language of Criticism* (London: Methuen, 1966).

3. See Maurice Mandelbaum, "Family Resemblances and Generalizations Concerning the Arts," *American Philosophical Quarterly* 2 (July 1965); George Dickie, *Art and the Aesthetic* (Ithaca: Cornell University Press, 1974); Ted Cohen, "The Possibility of Art: Remarks on a Proposal by Dickie," *Philosophical Review* 82 (1973): 69–82; and B. R. Tilghman, *But Is It Art?* (Oxford: Basil Blackwell, 1984). Further contributions to the investigation of the significance of Wittgenstein's philosophy for aesthetics are Richard Shusterman, "Wittgenstein and Critical Reasoning," *Philosophy and Phenomenological Research* 47 (September 1986); Richard Eldridge, "Problems and Prospects of Wittgensteinian Aesthetics," *Journal of Aesthetics and Art Criticism* 45 (Spring 1978); Carolyn Korsmeyer, "Wittgenstein and the Ontological Problem of Art," *The Personalist* 59 (April 1978); Roger A. Shiner, "The Mental Life of a Work of Art," *Journal of Aesthetics and Art Criticism* 40 (Spring 1982); Richard Wollheim, "The Art

make clear in this book, I believe the story to be vastly more complicated, and very much more philosophically and critically illuminating, than such a truncated narrative of philosophical progress would suggest.

The story that follows resists encapsulation, but I can say at least that, first, it does not seem to me true that the two areas of impact just mentioned in fact capture what is of greatest significance in Wittgenstein's philosophy for aesthetics and, second, it accordingly does not seem to be at all obvious that post-Wittgensteinian aesthetic theory is wiser in the way it should be if it wants to proceed as it does. So, although I do raise the issues of definition and aspect perception in this book, central to it are, rather, Wittgenstein's investigations into the nature, or natures, of meaning, especially where those investigations bear directly on our understanding of artistic and literary meaning. Thus I discuss the extent and the limit[4] of the relationship between aesthetic meaning and Wittgensteinian linguistic philosophy as well as the problems they have in common. I also try to sustain a sensitivity to the shaping influences on our

---

Lesson," in *On Art and the Mind* (Cambridge: Harvard University Press, 1974); P. B. Lewis, "Wittgenstein on Words and Music," *British Journal of Aesthetics* 17 (Spring 1977); Rush Rhees, "Art and Philosophy," in *Without Answers* (London: Routledge & Kegan Paul, 1969); Frank Cioffi, "When Do Empirical Methods Bypass 'The Problems Which Trouble Us'?" in *Philosophy and Literature*, Royal Institute of Philosophy Lectures, Vol. 16, ed. A. Phillips Griffiths (Cambridge: Cambridge University Press, 1984); Peter Winch, "Text and Context," in *Trying to Make Sense* (Oxford: Basil Blackwell, 1987); R. K. Elliott, "Imagination in the Experience of Art," in *Philosophy and the Arts*, Royal Institute of Philosophy Lectures, vol. 6, ed. Godfrey Vesey (London: Macmillan, 1973); and the collections of papers in *Inquiry* 31 (December 1989), and *New Literary History* 19 (Winter 1988). Also, since I completed this book, two other works have appeared that explore directions similar to some of those I take in Chapters 1 and 2; these are Karlheinz Lüdeking, "Pictures and Gestures," *British Journal of Aesthetics* 30 (July 1990); and B. R. Tilghman, *Wittgenstein, Ethics and Aesthetics* (London: Macmillan, 1991).

4. See, for example, Richard Wollheim's discussion of the discontinuities between artistic and linguistic meaning in *Painting as an Art* (Princeton: Bollingen, 1987), esp. chaps. 1, 2, and 4.

thinking about these topics in the very formulation of those problems. What, however, can be said of an introductory nature from a somewhat lower altitude?

Throughout aesthetics and literary criticism the use of emotive-descriptive terms and the conjoined philosophical problem of justifying such usage (where the fully articulated description of a work is often tantamount to a fully articulated interpretation of that work) have been undeniably central. Stated in terms that are familiar (but which are in fact, as we shall see, too philosophically stark to accommodate the facts of aesthetic practice), critical engagement with a work of art or literature generates descriptions that in turn demand justification; those then-justified descriptions, collected together, constitute an interpretation that should then (if we find the justification acceptable) shape our subsequent aesthetic experience.

The problem of justifying critical descriptions of a work, given form in this way, has led to ever more grand, and thus more general, theoretical construals of the relations between the critical perceptions in the mind of the beholder and the aesthetic object itself described by the articulation of those perceptions. This formulation of the problem presumes an aesthetic variant of metaphysical extensionalism, the belief that physical, extended objects are in both ontological and perceptual senses primary, so that we perceive only those objects directly or in an unmediated way; all other perceptions are thus taken to be indirect, mediated in a sense, and thus in need of justification. On this view, to put it simply, we see a bluish-green, but we only infer the nonextended or nonphysical quality of emotional depth. We read the words on the page, we only infer the human seriousness of the story. We hear a move from E to E-flat, we infer a darkening sense of foreboding. This view, which I hope to repudiate, has promoted ever greater levels of explanatory generality and an attendant disregard for detail, along with an insufficient grasp of the significance of such detail not only for critical practice but for the conjoined philosophical problem of critical justification.

In place of such an ascent to explanatory generality, we need, I believe, a descent, indeed of the sort exemplified in the late work of Wittgenstein, to the critically and aesthetically site-specific, contextually grounded details that generate emotive-descriptive usages in the first place and that themselves justify (in, as we shall see, a noninferential way) those aesthetic-linguistic practices. I attempt such a descent in Chapters 3, 4, and 5 of this book. First, however, I locate the ground, and this is the project of Chapters 1 and 2, in which I pursue Wittgenstein's answer to his own question that launched his later philosophy, "What is the meaning of a word?"[5]

The Wittgensteinian analytical strategy of the language-game, insofar as it affords an exquisitely detailed and controlled examination of the uses of words within delimited contexts, provides insight into expressive limits, stylistic integrity, organic cohesion, incremental developments of expressive capacities, and the instrumental employments of artistic materials within analogous aesthetic microcosms. In Chapter 1, I pursue such connections between the linguistic and the aesthetic, and this pursuit introduces the topics of Chapter 2, in which I first assemble an overview, a general conception, of the difficult phrase "a form of life" as it is employed in Wittgenstein's philosophy of language, and then proceed to a detailed consideration of cases within which thoughts and feelings are expressed in art as they are expressed through gesture and as they are embedded in ritualistic practices. The strikingly close relations, indeed the isomorphic parallels, between language-games and artistic styles, and between a form of life and a collection of artistic practices, lend new and positive content to

5. This is of course the opening question of Ludwig Wittgenstein, *The Blue and Brown Books* (Oxford: Basil Blackwell, 1958), p. 1.

the analogy between art and language, given a conception of language strikingly unlike those which have heretofore been influential—often misleadingly influential—throughout aesthetic theory.⁶ Taken together, then, the first two chapters are an attempt to respond to the need for a fairly detailed examination of Wittgenstein's later conception of linguistic meaning as a way of constructing a large-scale foundation for an understanding of Wittgensteinian criticism and literary epistemology. The particular issues that arise in these first chapters are the nature, scope, expressive limits, and expansions of language-games; the significance of context for meaning within language-games; the ideas of linguistic use, aim, and function and the significance of these for art; examples of artistic and literary language-games; linguistically engendered insights into aesthetic qualities such as coherence and inventiveness; the definition and understanding of the concept "form of life"; meanings resistant to propositional formulation and gestural significance; the notion of artistic "spirit"; aesthetic rule-following; and the relations between artistic uses and interpretative meaning.

In addition to answering the need for the descent to the level of detail, Wittgenstein's phrase "to imagine a form of life" carries an implicit invitation to turn to literary examples, which, with the particular case of the philosophical novelist Henry

---

6. I have discussed some of these conceptions of language as they have influenced aesthetic theory in a number of articles, to include: "Obviating Aesthetic Dualism," forthcoming in a collection on the work of Joseph Margolis edited by Lars Aagaard-Mogenson; "The Language of Feeling," forthcoming in the *Journal of Aesthetics and Comparative Literature*; "The Aesthetics of Indiscernibles," in *Visual Theory: Painting and Interpretation* (New York: Harper Collins, 1991), ed. Norman Bryson, Michael Ann Holly, and Keith Moxey; "Artistic Intention and Mental Image," *Journal of Aesthetic Education* 22 (Fall 1988): 63–75; "Creation as Translation," *Journal of Aesthetics and Art Criticism* 46 (Winter 1987): 249–58; "Music and Imagination," *Philosophy* 61 (October 1986): 513–17; "Art as Thought: The Inner Conflicts of Aesthetic Idealism," *Philosophical Investigations* 9 (October 1986): 257–93; and "Art and the Unsayable: Langer's Tractarian Aesthetics," *British Journal of Aesthetics* 24 (Autumn 1984): 325–40.

James,[7] the last three chapters of this book accept. Chapters 3 and 4 are investigations, via literary interpretation, into the varieties of linguistic meaning and the multiform moves made within the extended-yet-circumscribed language-games that constitute the Jamesian short story. The issues that arise here are the significance for linguistic philosophy of literary or, to be more specific, descriptively mimetic complexity; the circumstantial prerequisites for linguistic force; relations between aesthetic and ethical descriptions, by which I mean the very many ways we have of describing what we see in a work of art, what we see as the aesthetic aspects of an object or person, and what we see in the actions and the verbal and gestural expressions of a person that holds ethical value or significance; the fundamental analogies between the perception of works of art, of significant artifacts, and of persons; the misleading power—particulary in aesthetic and literary-critical contexts—of the distinction between perception and description; the inability of linguistic atomism to serve as a theory of meaning "beneath" literary interpretation; the significance of tone and silence for linguistic meaning; the irreducible complexity of aesthetic and critical descriptions, which is shown by their refusal to settle into traditional philosophical distinctions such as mind and matter, self and other, emotion and reason, inner and outer, and intrinsic and relational; the critical inapplicability of the all-too-familiar additive model (text plus interpretation) and its relation to Wittgenstein's discussion of aspect perception; perceptions, descriptions, and interpretations of human facial expressions and the "logic" of understanding facial expressivity; and the irreducibility of an aesthetic phenomenon as complex as literary meaning.

In Chapter 5 I extend the project of philosophical investi-

7. For this dimension of James's work, see Renford Bambrough, "Ounces of Example," in *Realism in European Literature: Essays in Honour of J. P. Stern*, ed. Nicholas Boyle and Martin Swales (Cambridge: Cambridge University Press, 1986).

gation through literary interpretation and attempt to show the contribution the Wittgensteinian method of investigation can make to a larger understanding of literature and its epistemological value. The issues that arise here are the problematic character of the distinction between philosophy as an analytical activity and philosophy as an interpretative or literary-critical activity; the pragmatic question of the significance for literary-critical practice of the Wittgensteinian analytical method; the limitations on critical-methodological encapsulation; the antisystematic diversity exhibited by the word "knowledge" and some of the categories of its usage; the vast range separating the spoken from the unspoken with regard to what one knows; the weaving of a fabric of simulated knowledge or self-deception; and, again, the prerequisite of detail to the achievement of a complex yet clarifying overview of a philosophically problematic concept such as knowledge.

Anyone who has read Wittgenstein should of course be wary of generalizations and, for that matter, of general remarks about the danger of generalizations. Nevertheless, to describe this project in general terms: I attempt to identify and elucidate Wittgenstein's nonreductive and contextualist views on meaning which hold special significance for our understanding of the experience of art and literature, and to show that significance through close readings (in what is perhaps a newly articulated sense of that phrase) of a writer whose fiction is itself one kind of epistemology.

1

∾ Language-Games and Artistic Styles

Wittgenstein introduces the idea of language-games to address the problems of truth and falsehood, the agreement of propositions with reality, and the nature, or natures, of assertions, assumptions, and the very act of questioning.[1] As there has been considerable disagreement over the definition and use of language-games, as well over the specific features of language and linguistic activity that they are designed to make salient, let us begin with Wittgenstein's own introductory remarks to this analytical tool. He says, "The study of language-games is the study of primitive forms of language or primitive languages."[2] Of course, by the time he'd developed this tool[3] he no longer believed that actual discourse was simply a rather messy affair that had to be cleaned up (that is, formalized into logical perfection) as he did earlier while working under the influence of Bertrand Russell, but rather that ordinary language

---

1. See the introductory discussion of this idea from which this list of issues is drawn, in Ludwig Wittgenstein, *The Blue and Brown Books* (Oxford: Basil Blackwell, 1958), pp. 17–20.

2. *Ibid*, p. 17.

3. That is to say, at this stage, Wittgenstein no longer regarded the referential perfection sought after in *Tractatus Logico-Philosophicus* as an ideal toward which philosophy should aspire.

was in fact extraordinarily complex, and that those intrinsic complexities are of a magnitude to obscure if not preclude our view of some of the fundamental features of language as it is used. Thus, he says, language-games are "ways of using signs simpler than those in which we use the signs of our highly complicated everyday language," and through language-games we can see, clearly if only partially, the complex "forms of thinking," as they appear in "primitive forms of language," in a very advantageous position, that is, "without the confusing background of highly complicated processes of thought." And indeed the remarkable thing about employing language-games within larger investigations into the nature of language is that inside the linguistic microcosms of these primitive forms of language "the mental mist which seems to enshroud our ordinary use of language disappears."

Naturally, any strategy that promises clarity is worth pursuing. But this must be approached in stages: the first is to look at Wittgenstein's own development of the language-game strategy in connection with the problem of linguistic meaning; the second is to identify the features of language this strategy renders evident; the last is to assess the results of an analogical employment of language-games in the arts and to see if any of the mist enshrouding the concept of artistic meaning has in fact disappeared.

The Concept of a Language-Game

Despite the unfortunate connotations of the word "game," a "language-game" is neither trivial ("only a game") nor primarily concerned with rule-following (playing "strictly according to the rules"). That language-games are not trivial can, of course, be seen only at the end of this discussion. That they are not concerned with the laying bare of the rule-governed nature of natural language can be addressed, at least in part, presently.

It is significant that Wittgenstein does not mention rules when introducing the idea of the language-game. Following the remark about clearing the mist, he says, "We see activities, reactions, which are clear-cut and transparent." And in the fully mature use of this idea in the early sections of *Philosophical Investigations*, it is the general idea of the meaning of a word, and the corresponding attempts to capture that meaning theoretically, which are identified as the source of the mist. Already looking back to section 1 of *Philosophical Investigations* and the much-discussed "five-red-apples" case, in which he imagines sending a person with a shopping list with the words "five red apples" written on it to a shopkeeper (who *acts* in a way, or *uses* the words in such a way, that no question of the meaning of the word "five" arises),[4] Wittgenstein says, "If we look at the example in Section 1, we may perhaps get an inkling how much this general notion of the meaning of a word surrounds the working of language with a haze which makes clear vision impossible." Making it very clear that it is indeed *clarity* he is after, he continues, "It disperses the fog to study the phenomena of language in primitive kinds of applications in which one can command a clear view of the aim and functioning of the words."[5] The topic of the aim and function of words is remote from the study of the rules according to which words may be uttered.[6] And it is a clear view of that aim and that function

---

4. Ludwig Wittgenstein, *Philosophical Investigations*, 3d ed., trans. G.E.M. Anscombe (New York: Macmillan, 1953), sec. 1; a preliminary sketch for this example can be found in *The Blue and Brown Books*, pp. 16–17.

5. *Philosophical Investigations*, sec. 5.

6. I use Wittgenstein's phrase "aim and function" throughout this discussion, but by it I do not mean that the speaker *deliberates* on the aim of a word either preceding its use or as it is used. A lung, for example, has a function, and, in a sense, an "aim", but not where its employment requires deliberation or intention; I discuss the removal of ratiocination from center stage in Chapter 2. My use of "aim" might, incidentally, be characterized as Aristotelian; at the beginning of the *Nicomachean Ethics* Aristotle identifies happiness as the aim of all human activity, but Aristotle still could not have meant that all human

within the context of the language-game under consideration which is desired. In the discussion of the case of the shopkeeper and the apples, the interlocutor tries, if only indirectly, to bring into consideration the question of rules, by asking, "But how does he know where and how he is to look up the word 'red' and what he is to do with the word 'five'?" Wittgenstein's response refocuses the issue on linguistic aim and function, saying, "Well, I assume that he *acts* as I have described."[7] And he adds at this very early point the remark that, as we shall see, is of the utmost importance to our understanding of language-games: "Explanations come to an end somewhere." The insistent interlocutor responds, "But what is the meaning of the word 'five'?" Wittgenstein, resisting the encroaching haze, says at this point simply, "No such thing was in question here, only how the word 'five' is used."

What shall we, then, expect so far? The language-game strategy will (1) make readily visible the *aims* and the *functions* of words; (2) show us the manageably miniscule context in which those words have aims and functions; (3) systematically prevent the fog-bound *general* question of the meaning of a word from arising; (4) disallow questions extraneous to the smaller and circumscribed context of the language-game, for example, the interlocutor's question pertaining, if only indirectly, to the rules under which the shopkeeper uses "five"; and (5) make us sensitive, in a way that we could not be in the extraordinarily complex contexts of actual language, to the lines demarcating the limits of those language-games and to verbal and conceptual transgressions of those limits. For the same reasons the employment of the language-game strategy will make us sensitive

---

action is immediately subsequent to deliberation about the employment of means to the end of happiness.

7. Although this remark does unfortunately create the impression of an underlying behaviorism and thus appears to support a common misunderstanding of Wittgenstein's antimentalism, it in fact makes salient, not actual behavior, but rather the action of a person *within* a context.

to every incremental expansion of the context in a way we could never be in full-scale discourse.

Let us pursue these matters. We are familiar with the idea that the meaning of a word is uniform and generally accurate regardless of local linguistic detail; Wittgenstein quotes Augustine's *Confessions* to this effect as the opening move of *Philosophical Investigations*.[8] In that view, language has an essence, words function as names, sentences or propositions are constituted by combining such names, and—very generally—the meaning of a word is the object for which it stands. With this background in mind Wittgenstein turns to the shopkeeper with the slip marked "five red apples." At a glance we can see, at least within this narrow context, that Augustine's conception is already in trouble. "Apples" might conform to this theory of meaning, although "apple" would be better. "Red" is more troublesome: does it *mean* what it stands for? Again, we might save the Augustinian definition of meaning, but only by going far beyond this language-game to speak of qualities, properties, and so on. And "five" is most troublesome, because its meaning cannot be derived from just looking at the apples. And in the middle of this theory-threatening introductory game Wittgenstein mentions that "it is in this and similar ways that one operates with words." "Ways," after all, is plural; and "naming" is only one operation performed with words. We have, inside this very narrowly delimited game, seen ostensive naming replaced by the more powerful idea of linguistic aim and function.

This replacement is further shown in the equally well known and even more discussed language-game of the builders, who work within the linguistic microcosm that includes only "block," "pillar," "slab," "beam"; here the meaning of the word "Slab!" could not be *only* the object to which "slab" refers. But the

8. It is worth remembering here that Wittgenstein does not for one moment agree with Augustine's position; indeed, he found it especially useful as a point of departure because he found it astonishing that so great a mind could have held it.

replacement is accomplished with greater finesse in section 6, in which Wittgenstein imagines children being taught the language of the builders. Here we have a teacher directing the child's attention to the slab, pointing at it, and saying "slab." Doesn't this vindicate the Augustinian conception of meaning? Isn't this a clear case of the meaning of a word being the thing for which it stands? Decidedly not, for to formulate the question itself is to transgress the limits of the game. Wittgenstein says, parenthetically, "I do not want to call this 'ostensive definition', because the child cannot as yet *ask* what the name is." That is to say, within this linguistic microcosm, the question, "What is that thing called?" that we might presume the child to have asked not only was not, but in fact *could* not, be asked; we are, again, inside the invented language-game "consisting of the words 'block', 'pillar', 'slab', 'beam' " (*PI*, sec. 2). Nevertheless, one might insist, on behalf of Augustine and the possibility of a general conception of meaning, that the case does "establish an association between the word and the thing" (*PI*, sec. 6). It may well be true, as Wittgenstein readily admits, that such an association is formed, and thus that uttering the word is like "striking a note on the keyboard of the imagination"; however, the point is that the function of the word "slab," within this rarified pedagogical language-game, is *not* to evoke a mental image. The Augustinian element, if present, still cannot capture the meaning. Indeed, one operates with words, and such operations, like moves in a game, are made possible by the context in which the move is made. And to move, to operate, is to act. Thus Wittgenstein says, in section 7, "I shall also call the whole, consisting of language and the actions into which it is woven, the 'language-game'." Many have thought of Wittgenstein's use of this analytical tool that, if it is a game, then one must play according to the *rules*. It appears that we would be closer to the intended use if we said, as Wittgenstein does elsewhere, "This game is *played*!"[9]

9. This, of course, reinforces the idea of a focus on action within a context

An increased sensitivity to the expansion of a language-game is another of the rewards of this strategy. Wittgenstein demonstrates this by adding, to the language-game of the builders, the designations A, B, C, and D; the words "there" and "this"; and a number of color samples. In this slightly expanded language-game, one builder might say to another, 'D-slab-there," while showing him a color sample and pointing to a particular location. With these few additions, a language-game has been created that is much more complex than its predecessor. The range of possible misunderstandings has been similarly increased. First, as we have seen before, the ostensive definition here of "A, B, C, and D" will not suffice, because an assistant could believe himself to be in control of these words having been shown one, two, three, and then four slabs, and then, on hearing "C-beam," find himself utterly lost. Worse, he might similarly equate "this" with a particular shape, say that of the block, and find himself utterly lost when it is used in conjunction with any other shape. The importance of aim and function—that is, *use*—is made clearer in the case of "there." Indeed, Wittgenstein puts the question as follows: "Are 'there' and 'this' also taught ostensively?—Imagine how one might teach their use" (*PI*, sec. 9). In fact, trying to teach the meaning of the word "there" ostensively would produce either ineradicable frustration, or perhaps to a different sensibility, unbounded hilarity, since *anything* pointed to is in fact "there." On ostension, Wittgenstein adds, "One will point to places and things—but in this case the pointing occurs in the *use* of the words too and not merely in learning the use" (*PI*, sec. 9). This last point is as powerful as it is condensed. The individual words may indeed be taught through ostension, but such *acts* of ostension, such "pointings," will in fact occur *within* the context of actual linguistic practice. The definition of the word, and the learning of its use, is not prior to the language-game inside which that

---

rather than on mere outward behavior; see also *Philosophical Investigations*, secs. 654–56.

word functions. And, indeed, it may well, and probably will, have multiple functions and uses, but this multiplicity will be determined by the context, the larger game, within which the word operates.

Nevertheless, one might still insist, in a way consistent with the traditional search for a general theory of meaning, that a word, even if taught ostensively within contextual limits, within a game with autonomous and internally generated ranges of possible moves, *must* have a meaning, that it must signify above and beyond any particular game. Thus in section 10 Wittgenstein entertains the question of what the words of the microcosmic language signify, and realizes that the significance has already been *shown*, in the use, and that the use has been described.[10] If we insist that "slab" signifies this object and not (say, to correct a mistake) that block-shaped one over there, then we have done something that looks like directly describing the significance of "slab." But this too is not, after all, context-free referential meaning, "because the kind of *'referring'* this is ... is already known" (*PI*, sec. 10). Thus the ability to state that the word "slab" signifies that particular object is rendered possible *within* the game; in this case to correct an error also made possible within it. And numerous further mistakes or possible misunderstandings within this microcosm can be corrected in a very similar way, that is, through ostensive pointing and "labeling." But it does not follow from the fact of the similarity of the descriptions of the uses of these few words that the aims and functions of the words *themselves* are similar.

The above observation is high on the list of philosophically relevant but easily forgotten facts, and it is made all the more perilously forgettable by the fact that words, "when we hear them spoken or meet then in script or print" (*PI*, sec. 11), exhibit a misleadingly uniform appearance. Taken together,

---

10. This section thus houses an implicit backward glance at the *Tractatus*, in which the comparison of the later with the earlier view further reinforces the position that the meaning has *already* been shown in the use.

words have a unitary look, their applications and functions—their powers—within contexts are obscured, and the similarity of the descriptions of their uses make them appear further alike. But because of the already multifarious ways we see language operating inside this slightly expanded builders' language-game, this uniformity is utterly fallacious, a mirage produced by superficial linguistic appearance. For these words and their functions are "as we see...absolutely unlike" (*PI*, sec. 10). From this vantage point it is then perhaps less puzzling than usual why Wittgenstein says, in section 13, "When we say 'Every word in language signifies something' we have so far said *nothing whatever*." Because of the context-free generality of this remark, I believe that Wittgenstein meant quite literally *nothing*. To be more precise, "Every word in language signifies something" is an empty statement because it can only be made above and beyond any language-game or context within which moves, or aims and functions, are possible. Of course, it could mean something, but only in a context in which, as Wittgenstein adds to this striking claim, "we have explained exactly *what* distinction we wish to make," for example, trying to explain to someone why Lewis Carroll's phrase "slithy toves" is in fact nonsense. A familiar Wittgensteinian slogan is that a word has meaning only in the context of a sentence. The claim that we have, in saying that every word signifies something, so far said *nothing* can be taken to suggest that a sentence has meaning only within a context. But with this thought we should now turn to a further consideration of what is perhaps the central reward of employing the language-game strategy, the increased sensitivity to the limits of the game.

Linguistic and Artistic Microcosms

It is easy to say and difficult to show that language-games, as employed by Wittgenstein, are internally circumscribed, and are thus autonomous, and that they also generate their own range of possible moves without transgressing their own boundaries, and are thus self-sufficient.[11] But Wittgenstein begins the task of showing the autonomous nature of language-games in section 19, in which he asks whether the call "Slab!" from the nonexpanded builders' language is a sentence or a word. If it is a word, then it certainly does not possess the same meaning as our word "slab" in ordinary language. Focusing on the instrumental function shows that "Slab!" is in that microcosmic language a *call*. And if this call "Slab!" is a sentence, then it is not, nor could it be, an instance of our elliptical sentence "Slab!" which is a truncated version of "Bring me a slab!" because there is "no such sentence" in this language-game (*PI*, sec. 19). Indeed, our "Bring me a slab!" cannot even be used to articulate the meaning of their "Slab!" because our sentence is not a possible maneuver within the narrowly described limits of their language.

At this juncture the debate with the interlocutor produces heat as well as light, and we must follow it closely. Wittgenstein adds to the above the seeming afterthought (which actually leads to his point), "But why should I not on the contrary have called the sentence 'Bring me a slab!' a *lengthening* of the sentence 'Slab!'?," thus suggesting a kind of linguistic relativity where neither their nor our language has Archimedean fixed points of meaning such that their locutions really mean some other in ours. They are independent and mutually autonomous. The interlocutor answers, "Because if you shout 'Slab!' you really mean: 'Bring me a slab!',", here illustrating the naive belief in a fixed point of linguistic reference, that any elucidation of their meaning will proceed in terms of our meaning. Wittgenstein asks, "But how do you do this: how do you *mean*

---

11. A helpful discussion of the self-sufficiency of language-games can be found in J. F. M. Hunter, " 'Forms of Life' in Wittgenstein's *Philosophical Investigations*," *American Philosophical Quarterly* 5 (October 1968): 233–43; reprinted in *Essays on Wittgenstein*, ed. E. D. Klemke (Urbana: University of Illinois Press, 1971).

that while you say '*Slab!*'? Do you say the unshortened sentence to yourself?" Within the context of this philosophical disagreement this argumentative salvo directed against the interlocutor is aimed directly at the presumed belief in the separability of meaning from saying, or of, in short, the conceptual prerequisite for the very kind of general theory of meaning with which we began. And showing that the function of this utterance is to explode that myth, he adds, "And why should I translate the call 'Slab!' into a different expression in order to say what someone means by it?" We might well answer that we should so translate because after all the separate utterances *mean* the same, although one occurs in the builders' linguistic microcosm and the other in our larger language, which would be reasonable if meaning and saying were separable. Wittgenstein does not delay in countering that answer: "... and if they mean the same thing—why should I not say: 'When he says "slab!" he means "slab"?' "

Of course, this translation, as mere repetition, is obviously worth precisely nothing as an explanation of meaning—yet such reduplication is what the interlocutor's demands, if fulfilled, seem to generate. And again suggesting a mutual autonomy between language-games, Wittgenstein asks, "Again, if you can mean 'bring me the slab', why should you not be able to mean 'Slab!'?" In what must be some admixture of desperation and exasperation, the interlocutor answers, "But when I call 'slab!', then what I want is, *that he should bring me a slab*!" And now placing before the eyes of the reader the inescapable absurdity of the interlocutor's mentalistic conception of the meaning the word is believed to have, Wittgenstein answers, "Certainly, but does 'wanting this' consist in thinking in some form or other a different sentence from the one you utter?" And must not someone who views linguistic meaning as something above and beyond the word, the sentence, and the context share the view of the interlocutor? If he views linguistic meaning as something that is fixed outside the language-game within which it allegedly later operates, and as something prior to its employment within the specific moves of a game, then indeed he is in perfect harmony with the interlocutor. Wittgenstein, however, rejects this view, claiming rather that meanings are *native* residents of their contexts, of particular regions of language.

In conjunction with the autonomy of language-games there exists the issue of self-sufficiency or the idea that possible moves are internally generated and that language-games consequently define their own boundaries. And, of course, if the possible moves of the language-game are equivalent to what, cumulatively, that language-game has a capacity to express, and if the boundaries or limits of a language-game, as the far reaches of those moves, demarcate the line between the linguistically expressible on the one side and the unintelligible, ineffable, or unsayable on the other, then these features of Wittgenstein's strategy ought not to come as a surprise.[12]

A fundamental question at this point is, when a speaker in a linguistic microcosm utters an expression within it, whether the *other* available utterances of that microcosm must be in some sense present to the mind of the utterer. Wittgenstein's own answer to this question casts much light on his larger concept of language-games. If a builder says, "Bring me a slab," he could, the interlocutor suggests in section 20, "mean this expression as one long word corresponding to "Slab!" The interlocutor is of course looking back to the previous discussion, but Wittgenstein moves ahead by asking, "How does one usually mean it?" and answers his own question by saying that when we use it in contrast with other sentences available within this expanded builder's language, such as "*Hand* me a slab," or "Bring *him* a slab," or "Bring *two* slabs," and so on, then we

---

12. The strict demarcation of the bounds of the intelligible is of course the objective of the *Tractatus*. A discussion of the attempt to build an aesthetic theory that foundation can be found in my "Art and the Unsayable: Langer's Tractarian Aesthetics," *British Journal of Aesthetics* 24 (Autumn 1984): 325–40.

would say that we mean the initial command as four words. But the important point here rests not with the counting of words; it is rather that we use those four words, within the expanded linguistic microcosm, "in contrast with sentences containing the separate words of our command in other combinations." We are thus here introduced to the idea of multiple combinations and permutations resident within the language-game, an idea that lends content to the larger conception of the self-sufficiency of language-games.

Immediately germane, however, are the interlocutor's following questions: "But what does using one sentence in contrast with others consist in? Do the others, perhaps, hover before one's mind? *All* of them? And *while* one is saying the one sentence, or before, or afterwards?" These questions are grounded in the very sort of context-free linguistic mentalism that Wittgenstein is opposing or, better, precluding; and illustrating the philosophical practice of looking to see, he replies, "No. Even if such an explanation rather tempts us, we need only think for a moment of what actually happens in order to see that we are going astray here." To clarify what for our immediate concern is most important, the self-sufficiency of language-games, that is, how they generate their own expressive or locutionary possibilities, he adds, "We say that we use the command in contrast with other sentences because our language contains the possibilities of those other sentences." Here Wittgenstein has moved from context-free mentalism, where minds hold expressive potentialities irrespective of context, to the context of the language-game itself. The limits of the expressible are *not* mentally or solipsistically drawn; they are a function of the possible moves of the game. The builder, who sees clearly this multiplicity of expressive possibilities, the web of "Hand or Bring, me or him, a or two, slab or slabs," and so on, has what Wittgenstein refers to a bit later in the same section as "a *mastery* of this language," and he makes clear that this language, the expanded builders' language, "contains those other sentences as well—but is this having a mastery something that *happens* while you are uttering the sentence?" We shall return to this concept of mastery because it will prove to be one of the clearest points of intersection between art and language. But before progressing to the discussion of the dimensions of art perfectly corresponding to, and thus in fact constituting, stylistic language-games, there remain a few more characteristics of language-games that must be identified first.

In section 22 of *Philosophical Investigations* Wittgenstein sounds a cautionary note concerning the unwitting transgression of the limits of a language-game. He observes that although Frege believed that every assertion could be characterized, or written in the form, "It is asserted that such-and-such is the case," in fact, " 'that such-and-such is the case' is *not* a sentence in our language," thus suggesting that the attempt to characterize assertion *generally* in a context-free form is in an interesting way impossible. Assertion, after all, takes place as an action embedded within the game, and its attempted general characterization occurs, naturally, above and beyond it. Indeed, we are here inclined to transgress the limits—the context—that assure the intelligibility of the assertion in the first place. "So far," Wittgenstein adds, "it is not a *move* in the language-game." Still, illegitimate moves in a language-game are only part of Wittgenstein's concern here. If we claim, as a further manifestation of a desire to give the act of propositional assertion a general formulation, that by saying, "Such-and-such is the case," we really mean, "It is asserted: such-and-such is the case," then the "words 'it is asserted' simply become superfluous." And this gives us an example of a linguistic maneuver that *looks* like a legitimate move but is in fact vacuous or, indeed, superfluous. Such a prefatory phrase, dropped in from above, is again not a move *in* the game. In short, on the linguistic side of the analogy between language and art for which we have been laying the foundation, there are illusory "moves," or formulations, that look good but in fact are empty. And as we shall see below, there exists a direct parallel in art.

The final characteristic of language-games of which we must make note concerns not a sensitivity to but rather the nature of their expansion or growth. In section 23, referring to the multiplicity of kinds of sentences, Wittgenstein observes that this multiplicity "is not something fixed, given once for all; but new types of language, new language-games, as we may say, come into existence, and others become obsolete and get forgotten." Such growth is probably best characterized as "organic," which underscores the fact that the individuation of games is by no means a simple or predictable matter, and that individuation, insofar as it is called for at all, will proceed in different ways and according to different criteria in individual cases. And as we shall see, stylistic border disputes in the arts indicate that individuation is not a simple or straightforward matter in the analogous aesthetic contexts in which "organic" stylistic expansion occurs.[13] Moreover, this way of putting it shows one of the conceptual interrelations between the notions of language-games and "forms of life" as they appear in Wittgenstein's philosophy generally.[14] But the important point

---

13. Here again see J. F. M. Hunter, " 'Forms of Life.' "
14. That interrelations exist between the notions of "forms of life" and "language-games" does not of course entail that they are identical. For a discussion of games played with language, as "an obvious transition between childhood games and literature," see Laurence Lerner, *The Frontiers of Literature* (Oxford: Basil Blackwell, 1988), pp. 191–95. For an instance of a rule being first made explicit and then broken, bent, or altered as an artistic gesture, see the discussion from which this passage is taken: "Play sticks to the rules, play breaks the rules. Sticking to the rules of the game is what licenses the flouting of more serious rules. Simply to utter a row of incomprehensible syllables would not constitute much of a release, since it is so cheaply purchased: it offers no kind of threat to serious thinking" (Lerner, *Frontiers*, p. 200). For an analogous discussion in the visual arts, see Kirk Varnedoe, *A Fine Disregard: What Makes Modern Art Modern* (New York: Abrams, 1990), in which Varnedoe's governing insight is the fine, i.e., innovative, expressive, cultivated, and his-

24   *Meaning & Interpretation*

within the present context, that is, in establishing the expectations for what an account of artistic style will look like when elucidated as an analogue to language-games, is that language-games can grow, as do cities, in different ways at different times. In section 18, Wittgenstein shows that the concept of "completeness" is in fact alien to a discussion of language-games. Was our language, he asks, complete before the symbolism of chemistry or the notation of the infinitesimal calculus? There is, of course, no *fixed* number of houses and streets definitionally prerequisite for a town to be a town. Indeed, Wittgenstein makes this illuminating simile explicit in a well-known passage, saying, "Our language can be seen as an ancient city: a maze of little streets and squares, of old and new houses, and of houses with additions from various periods; and this surrounded by a multitude of new boroughs with straight regular streets and uniform houses."[15] As we shall also see, artistic styles are similarly organic, completeness is foreign to them (and thus the specific conditions for their establishment are equally resistant to quantification), and they are, sometimes like medieval villages and sometimes like LeCorbusier's design for the razing and rebuilding of Paris, sites for multifarious developments.

Style, Coherence, and Artistic Limits

It seems clear that the multiplicity of language-games is itself crucial to an understanding of how they are meant to be employed within the philosophy of language, and in section 24 of *Philosophical Investigations* Wittgenstein says, "If you do not keep the multiplicity of language-games in view you will perhaps be

---

torically progressive disregard for the rules (in which the breaking of an old rule is coincident with the making of a new one).

15. For a discussion of Wittgenstein's use of the metaphor of language as a city, see Robert John Ackermann, *Wittgenstein's City* (Amherst: University of Massachusetts Press, 1988).

inclined to ask questions like: 'What is a question?' "[16] This remark is made following the list of language-games in section 23, which he prefaces by saying, "Review the multiplicity of language-games in the following examples, and in others." His intent is, of course, to illustrate the practice of *looking* at actual diversity instead of *thinking* about illusory uniformity. As a way of moving the discussion from language to art, we might first find examples in the arts analogous to Wittgenstein's multifarious list of language-games.

Although a very great number of such cases could be described, I suggest only a few for each entry on the list from section 23:

1. "Giving orders, and obeying them." In music, we make a certain aspect of a military march salient if we liken it to the giving of orders. And to march in step is to obey the beat if not the letter, of the rhythmically given order. In literature, a far more detailed case could be developed through a close reading of Henry James's notebooks, in which he gave himself "orders," like literary prescriptions, which in very many cases he followed later in the tales and novels.

2. "Describing the appearance of an object, or giving its measurements." The Rouen Cathedral series of Claude Monet, in which the subject remains constant but the presentation of it changes under varying lighting conditions, is such a description of appearance. One might think of the entire Dutch seventeenth-century still-life school as exemplifying and then organically expanding this move.[17] Visual art rarely "gives mea-

---

16. Although recognizing multiplicity can erode our confidence in questions of the "What is a question?" type and promote in us a healthy disrespect for essentialistic uniformity, acknowledging multiplicity certainly need not commit us to a subjective relativism about what may and may not be taken as a question, an answer, or the possibility of an answer. In this connection, see Renford Bambrough, "Unanswerable Questions," *Proceedings of the Aristotelian Society* supp. vol. 40 (1966): 151–72.

17. For the definitive argument that this entire movement was the exacting pursuit of *appearances* rather than the encoding of readable "meanings" char-

surements" but it does most assuredly depict dimension, examples being the sublimity of Alpine scenes, and the monumentality of Nature generally, in nineteenth-century Romantic painting. Describing the appearance of an object is also, of course, a game that is played throughout literature; we will consider particular cases of this, particularly where the descriptions of domestic interiors and of character function in very similar ways, below.

3. "Constructing an object from a description (a drawing)." One here thinks instantly of the famous Dürer illustration of the rhinoceros,[18] full of inaccuracies but, indeed, constructed from descriptions. Some of Leonardo's sketches for inventions, such as the helicopter, are similarly drawings of objects (in this case nonexistent) from his own prior descriptions. If we greatly expand the game to include "constructing a sense of a person's character and motivations," then again this game is played throughout fiction, as in the example of Henry James's character Peter in "The Tree of Knowledge," discussed in Chapter 5.

4. "Reporting an event." Narrative paintings of course provide countless examples, but in medieval painting the depiction of scenes of martyrdom serve nicely, as do many other forms and genres such as the Bayeux Tapestry reporting the details of battle, Trajan's column reporting Roman political events, and every Madonna and Child depiction. Political journalism is a nonartistic version of this language-game; when this game is represented in fiction, it itself is "reported" on, within the context of a work of art. Of course here too countless cases are readily available in fiction; we will return to some in detail in James's "The Author of Beltraffio."

5. "Speculating about an event." David's *Death of Marat* depicts an event the painter did not witness, and is thus specu-

---

acteristic of the southern art of the period, see Svetlana Alpers, *The Art of Describing* (Chicago: University of Chicago Press, 1983).

18. See Norman Bryson's discussion of this case in *Vision and Painting: The Logic of the Gaze* (New Haven: Yale University Press, 1983), pp. 22–25.

lative. More recently, many of Cindy Sherman's photographs of herself in multiple guises in divergent contexts can be construed as speculations on selves that might have been. In a different way, works of art and architecture can prompt speculations about events; consider Egyptian pyramids or Roman aqueducts. In fiction, the entire genre of the historical novel defines the context within which such speculation becomes possible.

6. "Forming and testing an hypothesis." One might say that the Impressionist movement, when it moved out of the studios and into the fields, was a painterly response to a hypothesis about the immediacy of vision and human perception;[19] the test was conducted, with ultimately successful results, with pigment on canvas.[20] One might say that artists test hypotheses about themselves in their capacity for creation within specific contexts as well, for example Gaugin's excursions to Tahiti or Stravinsky's to Hollywood. In ethics, we—to cast the matter only slightly oddly—form and test hypotheses in the process of coming to understand another person; this process becomes artistic when it is depicted and simultaneously commented on in fiction, as we shall see it done in James's "The Figure in the Carpet."

7. "Presenting the results of an experiment in tables and diagrams." Although tables and diagrams admittedly seem remote from artistic contexts, the presentation of experimental results is common throughout the arts. Arnold Schönberg's early twelve-tone works, Karlheinz Stockhausen's early uses of tape-splicing techniques in the studio, and John Cage's use of aleatory compositional procedures will serve. In a different way, Jackson Pollock's "psychoanalytic" paintings can be seen

---

19. See Richard Shiff, *Cezanne and the End of Impressionism* (Chicago: University of Chicago Press, 1984).

20. On the counterintuitive yet accurate placement of the model of scientific experimentation within artistic creation, see John Gilmour, *Picturing the World* (Albany: State University of New York Press, 1986).

as the results of a psychological experiment; Marcel Proust's novels can also be seen as a presentation of the results of a psychological experiment, one in which a conception of the self, its history, its continuities and discontinuities, and its engagements are created in the observation, in the self's literary depiction.

8. "Making up a story; and reading it." The morally deep visual narratives of Nicolas Poussin are in a sense "made-up"; "reading" a story can be reading a story, or painting a story, or acting out a story. "Reading" a music-drama (of any sort) entails every sort of reading except reading as narrowly construed, yet reading it is. Children's books are made up, and then illustrated; in a more sophisticated but still linguistically analogous way, Hogarth's engraving series, as moral stories invented and depicted, follow the same pattern. Of course, all of these cases are more examples of, rather than parallels to, Wittgenstein's language-game: they were aesthetic games to begin with.

9. "Play-acting." The eighteenth-century convention of English portraiture, in which subjects are depicted in costumes of remote times and places in order to associate ideas from apparel to the subject, or to reveal some aspect of the character of the subject, serves as a visual analogue. The distinction between oratorio and opera is also of use here; a performer plays the role of the character in the latter and not in the former. Of course, theater and film are perhaps the most obvious artistic exemplifications of this kind of language-game, but they do certainly appear in fiction. One case is James's character Mrs. Mallow, the wife of the artist who is (probably, as we shall see) playing a part with respect to what she does and does not know about Mr. Mallow.

10. "Singing catches." In learning to sing catches, or when participating in the singing of a round, what one learns is analogous to learning a verbal language of a technical discipline, for example, the terminology and nomenclature of harmonic

analysis. In singing a round, one learns, through making moves in the musical game, to come in at the right part, and once having successfully made the entrance (after a number of erroneous attempts), one learns to persist in one's own melody, despite what others are singing. The singing is indeed rule-governed, or at least stands in correspondence to rules, but one *plays* the game first, and one comes to hear what to do—what moves to make—through repeated trying and correcting, through action. And of course, even more directly than in the case of speech, the voice is used instrumentally.

11. "Guessing riddles." Works that represent riddles directly, such as Poussin's *Arcadian Shepherds*, the riddle of the Sphinx, and the entire genre of the spy novel spring to mind. But these are cases of riddles inside the narrative or pictorial context of the work itself. Beyond this, in many cases the perceiver of the work is placed in the position of the riddle-guesser, for example, the emotive content of the much-speculated-about enigmatic smile of the Mona Lisa, the Op-movement (as in "What is this one supposed to do?"), and the experience of coming face-to-face with a perfectly portrayed Campbell's soup can. And beyond this, many works seem to exude an undeniable yet inexplicable sense of depth and mystery, for example, Rothko's chapel paintings or, in very different ways, the *film noir* photographic technique or the control of light in early Romanesque churches. Of course the phrase "guessing riddles" aptly fits more than one character in "The Figure in the Carpet," a literary language-game to which we shall also return.

12. "Making a joke; telling it." When Goya was commanded to paint the portraits of the royal family, as a way of personally expressing his views of the family he portrayed them with stupefied facial expressions. And to the extent that those bovine gazes were discussed at all, they were understood as the best his technique would allow; that is, they were not seen as the deliberate moves in a game that they in fact were. In short, a visual joke was made and told. In a different way, the archi-

tectural jokes of Giulio Romano are clear to someone who knows the language—and the range of possible gestures within the visual vocabulary—of the Renaissance style of facade decoration. The rapidly descending figure that opens Stravinsky's *History of a Soldier* is undeniably comedic in its timbre as it descends into the lowest register and in its instrumentation. Examples of this language-game in literature are simply too numerous to mention.

13. "Solving a problem in practical arithmetic." If a bridge, as a work of architecture, can be a work of art, then the problems solved in, for example, Benjamin Baker's Forth Bridge provide a perfect illustration.[21] Of course, the solution of countless problems of structural engineering precede any architectural construction; cases such as the development of the flying buttress of the Gothic style or the employment of the cantilever in Frank Lloyd Wright's Falling Water render such accomplishments more visible to the critical eye. Another illustration can be found in the solving of problems of harmonization that occur in a fugue, where a composer desires to make not only correct but rather the best possible moves within the fugue's thematic logic.

14. "Translating from one language into another." Throughout his work, but perhaps most notably in the string quartets, Bartok incorporated Hungarian folk themes, or fragments of those themes, into the much larger-scale compositional structure of the quartet. Simply put, he translated motifs from one idiom into another. Mussorgsky's *Pictures at an Exhibition* is a different kind of translation, this time across the arts. In a

---

21. For the detailed discussion of these contextually situated problems, see Michael Baxandall, *Patterns of Intention* (New Haven: Yale University Press, 1985), pp. 12–40. See also in this connection Mary Mothersill's discussion of El Greco and the *Count Orgaz* case, in which it is made clear that the context of the lines of the painting determines the aesthetic significance of those lines, in *Beauty Restored* (Oxford: Clarendon Press, 1984), chap. 11, "The Concept of Beauty: Aesthetic Properties," pp. 323–66.

similar way Debussy captures in translation an aspect of nature in *La Mer*. Rilke's *Letters on Cezanne*[22] can easily be construed as yet another kind of translation, in this case the visual to the verbal. Reversing the direction of translation, a filmmaker begins with a script and ends with its visual realization. Further, within music, a full orchestration of a piece originally composed for piano or small ensemble and the reduction to a piano score of an orchestral piece are strikingly like translations. Moreover, debates concerning the quality and accuracy of such transcriptions mirror perfectly debates concerning the quality and accuracy of translations.

15. "Asking, thanking, cursing, greeting, praying." Charles Ives's *Unanswered Question* is aptly titled. The brass ask one question over and over, and receive increasingly full but ultimately unsatisfying "answers." Thanking has a definite place within the musical structure of the mass, as well as within the visual context of, for example, late medieval painting. In a very different way, sculptural works commissioned for commemoration, for example, of Winston Churchill, are sculpturally embodied gestures of thanks. Depictions of cursing, as might be imagined, are common among illustrations of Dante's *Divine Comedy*; cursing also occurs in a vividly literal way in the more authentic variants of blues music. Greeting, in the arts, is perhaps best exemplified in architecture; it is difficult to think of a clearer case than that of the enveloping curved "arms" of the colonnade of the courtyard of St. Peter's Cathedral. Similarly, almost any successful portico in secular architecture achieves the same effect, if perhaps not so forcefully. Praying can be found in the arts in a number of very different ways; it is given a context and is encouraged by the traditions of interior design in sacred architecture, it is encouraged or visually depicted in painting, and it is given occasion again within the setting of the

---

22. Rainer Maria Rilke, *Letters on Cezanne*, trans. Joel Agee (New York: Fromm International, 1986).

mass. Moreover, although this is not the place to pursue the topic, some would argue that there are phenomenological interconnections between religious and aesthetic experience quite generally.

Wittgenstein assembled this list to remind us that those who insist that there are really only three fundamental kinds of sentence, assertion, question, and command, are wrong, that there are in fact "*countless* kinds: countless different kinds of use of what we call 'symbols', 'words', 'sentences'." And, like the growth of a city, "this multiplicity is not something fixed." At the end of the list Wittgenstein remarks, "It is interesting to compare the multiplicity of the tools in language and of the ways they are used, the multiplicity of kinds of word and sentence, with what logicians have said about the structure [and essence] of language." and he includes among these logicians the author of the *Tractatus Logico-Philosophicus*. After even a brief review of the analogous language-games in art, it is equally interesting to compare this multiplicity with what aestheticians have said about the structure and essence of art. We saw Wittgenstein's remark concerning the importance of keeping the multiplicity within the philosophy of language in clear view; failing to do so, he warns, will generate "questions like: What is a question?" where what is asked for is a general account that captures the essence of a question quite apart from the context within which the specific question arises and quite apart from the aim and function of that question. We might also ask, if we fail to keep artistic multiplicity in clear view, questions such as "What is a painting?" which may mean "What [essentially] must every painting have to be a painting?" or "What [instrumentally] must every painting in fact do to be a painting?" and expect an answer that is "correct" regardless of any particular context. And even if questions such as "What is art?" are generally regarded as being hopelessly general, questions such as "What is music?" "What is film?" "What is architecture?" and so on often are not, but the latter questions attempt to operate above and beyond a language-game in which intelligibility is ensured, just as does the question "What is a question?" Tools from a toolchest do not have a use outside the specific contexts within which they are employed; to ask for such a definition is to imply that they are *used generally*, which is an obvious absurdity. Cities do not grow and change *generally*; they do so on specific sites, and to suggest or imply anything else is equally obviously absurd. If these analogies are helpful in understanding language and if language is in turn helpful in understanding art, then we should be wary of aesthetic questions possessing the same generality and potentially the same absurdity. But this brings us to still another characteristic of language-games, their power to make visible, within restricted contexts, the limits of coherence, and we should now pursue the parallel in art.

We saw in the preceding section how easy it is to transgress the limits of a game unwittingly, to attempt to make a linguistic move not possible within circumscribed limits. In section 27 Wittgenstein reminds us of this, looking back to both the basic and the expanded builders' languages and saying of them that "there was no such thing as asking something's name. This, with its correlate, ostensive definition, is, we might say, a language-game on its own." In the arts, it is, even if difficult to say why, remarkably easy to recognize an analogous transgression. If in music we use parallel fifths to harmonize a chorale melody, that move will be instantly recognizable as a mistake—within this style. It is not simply a misplaced dissonance and thus a "simple" mistake; it is in fact too consonant. But listeners will hear that passage as out of place, as, indeed, a move not available to that game. Similarly, if an architect places a gothic window next to a romanesque, then places a series of oculi between a row of classical columns, and then supports an outer wall with a single gothic buttress countered by a baroque staircase on the opposite side, we know at a glance that the result is, quite simply, visually incoherent. Each of the architectural elements, as part of a larger design-vocabulary, implies the existence of other possible moves consistent with and afforded by that vocabulary, but these are, in this imaginary case of architectural incoherence, *not* the moves made. A range of possible moves is implied, analogues to "Hand me a slab," "Hand him a slab," "Hand her two slabs," and so on, but instead of such possible moves we get the visual equivalent of what is referred to in some quarters as a word salad. This is of course not to say that the demands of coherence preclude growth. We can see in retrospect the progressive visual invention, the clear expansion of a style in a manner that does not strain coherence, in the classical orders. The rather stern Doric yields to the softer Ionian, which in turn is expanded—but expanded within the same visual language—by the Corinthian. And indeed, like the synthesis of a few resident linguistic possibilities of a given game,[23] there followed the composite order. Similarly, postmodern architectural design incorporates sectors of various, previously established vocabularies, but does so, at least in the successful cases, in ways avoiding incoherence of the type imagined above; that we can tell the difference between the suc-

---

23. For a succinct example of the successful merger of two initially separate language-games, in which the linguistic moves of the synthesized game become themselves naturalized, see G. P. Baker and P. M. S. Hacker, *Wittgenstein: Understanding and Meaning* (Chicago: University of Chicago Press, 1980), p. 98: "Compare, e.g., the penetration of the hydrodynamic terminology into electrodynamics in virtue of the complex analogies between the behaviour of fluids and electricity. We all speak of 'electric *current*' (or of electricity as 'current'); and it is immediately intelligible to characterize voltage as electrical pressure or amperage as the rate of flow of electricity." For an analogous case in art, see Kirk Varnedoe on Rodin, where he discusses in detail how Rodin made in his sculpture new moves of completion and incompletion in the interest of generating new sculptural meanings, in *A Fine Disregard*, pp. 127–141. And for a clear statement, visually supported, of the significance of *use* within a delimited context for the determination of artistic meaning, see pp. 178–80. See also Richard Wollheim's discussion of Adrian Stokes, particularly on gesture and expression, in *On Art and the Mind* (Cambridge: Harvard University Press, 1974), esp. pp. 321–34.

cessful cases and the others so quickly is itself further, implicit endorsement of the analogy with language.

Naturally, the adjudication of the legitimacy of all moves made within stylistic languages, and specifically in merging or synthesizing such languages, is often controversial; for example, one can debate whether or not Gershwin ought to have merged musical idioms as he did, whether classical images ought to be used in advertising, whether Bach ought to be used as a basis for jazz improvisation, whether advertising icons, such as Brillo boxes or Campbell's soup cans, ought to be elevated to the status of objets d'art, whether Rauschenberg ought to have invented the antimove by erasing de Kooning, and so on. But in each of these cases, what is debated is the legitimacy of the move and whether or not the move is in fact generated within the style's vocabulary or what that style allows vis-à-vis logical expansion. In short, the very conception of artistic purity is elucidated in terms of what is "sayable," with propriety, within the boundaries of a style, just as debates about coherence and stylistic integrity are debates about the locations of the limits of artistic language-games and the justifiability of the mergers of such games.

The builders show that they understand a move in their game when they see how the linguistic move is meant to operate, or when they see its aim and function. When an audience member hears that a pianist displays the limits that the composer has circumscribed in the theme, and then when he hears, or beyond that comprehends, that the first variation is a move or set of moves made possible by that theme, mere brute perception becomes musical understanding. When he next hears that the second theme is an exploration of melodic, harmonic, or rhythmic possibilities generated by the initial theme and its first variation, its first controlled expansion of the language, he then understands that further dimension of the composition as well. Similarly, we can recognize the language to which "Girder!" might well be quite coherently added, and we can imagine how the builders would quickly come to use it. In a parallel fashion, many are able to recognize at a glance that a heretofore unseen painting is a painting by Cezanne by recognizing Cezanne's characteristic moves—particular moves we have not seen executed before but which nonetheless quite clearly belong to his style. In the same way one is able to imagine how Cezanne might have portrayed the exterior of one's own house with a certain volumetric or block-like aspect with distinctive shades of blue, green, and a range of colors in between. Moreover, recognizing the appropriateness of a move within Cezanne's style made by another painter is recognizing Cezanne's influence on that painter. And that it is a stylistic language-game we are perceiving is rendered further evident by the fact that we can recognize unexpected affinities between radically divergent styles, for example, between primitivism and modern art, as a function of seeing first the inner coherence of each style and then seeing that moves made within these styles, although irrevocably different for their differing contextual placements, are nevertheless in one specific aspect or another strikingly alike. And the appropriation of language-games for aesthetic purposes is still further warranted by the fact that we can, as we do indeed often describe it, "learn the language" of a given artist. Modigliani uses hard black lines to depict faces; Seurat uses concatenations of points of color. Debussy uses parallel harmonies and chords of the ninth, Stravinsky uses modernistic-yet-primitive rhythms. In these cases, one can very quickly recognize that what one is seeing or hearing is characteristic of that artist's style. One has learned, or at least learned to recognize, that artist's visual or auditory language.

Another centrally important characteristic of language-games in Wittgenstein is, as we saw above, their self-sufficiency or internal containedness, which is to say that the moves possible, the limits of the expressible within a language-game, are determined from within. To pursue this characteristic in art,

Language-Games and Artistic Styles 37

the case that most readily presents itself is that of serial or twelve-tone musical composition.

Traditional harmony possesses, as a centrally significant move, the establishment of key centers, such that a given work, movement, section, or passage is *in* a particular key. The first move of a serial composition is to repudiate key-centeredness, or traditional tonality, by requiring moves that intrinsically prevent the establishment of a key center. Very simply stated, a composer begins by defining a "row," a sequence of all twelve pitches of the chromatic scale, usually arranged in such a way to avoid implying a key center, which is usually accomplished by avoiding rising or falling intervals of a fourth or fifth. This row, intrinsically ambiguous harmonically in that it does not imply a tonic, is then permutated for the generation of other possible moves; these include playing the row backward (the retrograde row), upside-down (the inverted row), or both (the retrograde-inverted row). Already, although no real music has been composed, the composer has located within a compositional set of possibilities a set of moves generated and legitimated internally—and excluded a far larger set of moves, those associated with traditional harmony, which are by definition beyond the realm of the intelligible within this compositional system, because, as this is *serial* composition, each pitch must be employed in sequence. An entire row, if started, must be exhausted before any pitch may be employed a second time; thus one cannot simply choose desired pitches and establish a key. This language began with Schönberg, but as it evolved in the hands of Berg, Webern, the followers of the Second Viennese School, and up to and beyond Boulez in more recent years, it was both explored for its expressive range and intrinsic potentialities and expanded through the gradual subjection to serial ordering of other compositional parameters, such as dynamics, instrumentation, timbre, and more recently, within the context of the electronic studio, left-to-right and foregroundto-background sonic placement. Thus the composer first establishes the compositional language-game, the initial vocabulary, then expands the ranges of moves within it through recombinations that are themselves determined by the initial row, and then—having set the bounds of the "sayable" within this musical language not from without but from within through establishing the intrinsic combinatorial reach of the available vocabulary—begins to create a serial work.

From the listener's point of view, numerous phenomena occur which are perfect analogues to the experience of the hearer of a language-game. The piece can sound cacophonous to those who have not yet, in any sense, learned the language—just as "Slab!" is an inarticulate shriek to a nonbuilder. But if one is given the row, and then plays it at the piano a number of times (again, not the composition itself, but merely the row that generates the possible moves utilized within the composition) and then listens again, what was seemingly utterly incoherent begins to take on an elusive kind of sense. If one then plays the row at the piano in its retrograde, inverted, and retrograde-inverted forms, and listens again, incoherence is increasingly replaced by intelligibility. One has carried out the musical equivalent of not just gazing uncomprehendingly at the builders from afar but of *working* with them so that the aim and function of their language becomes comprehensible. And as one might follow the incremental expansions to the builders' language, so one can follow, through the integration of the dynamic range into serial ordering, the development and consequently expanded expressive range, of the serial technique. And, as is true with the language-game, at no point does one go *outside* the system to render it comprehensible, nor at any point on the way from perceived cacophony to musical understanding does one ask a question concerning the *general* nature of organized pitch any more than one asks about the general nature of a question devoid of context. Of course, one might ask a general question about *this* style, specifically if it precludes authentic compositional creativity through imposing a deterministic system on a composer who would otherwise possess an unhampered free will.[24] But the answer would be spelled out in particulars; for example one might examine the perfected musical microcosms created by Webern within the larger confines of serialism. This would also begin to demonstrate that the mastery of a style involves the capacity to see and to use to great effect moves that are available within the style and yet far from obvious. In any event, it is perhaps Webern's short works that demonstrate that serial composition, as an exact analogue to a language-game, is a self-generating and self-sufficient system.

Quite beyond this single musical case, one can easily imagine countless further illustrations of the correspondence between language-games and artistic styles. In Philip Johnson's glass house one can quickly learn, within that microcosm of the modernist vocabulary, which moves are possible and which are not. In southern German baroque churches one can see quite quickly how alien a monastic darkness would be to that style. In St. Mark's in Venice, one can see some "Eastern" gestures. Indeed, St. Mark's is a very specific site for stylistic expansion through merger; the (recognition of) Byzantine influence is an instance of (the recognition of) stylistic merger. And in the paintings of Philip Guston one can see a return from an abstract language, with its intrinsic delimitations, to figuration, which brings a range of possible gestures obviously unavailable to the language of abstraction. In Anselm Keifer one sees the definition of a number of sites for expansion; these include the integration of non-oil textures, for example, that of molten metal, onto the canvas, and the heavily textured series of "books," which obscure the distinction between painting and

---

24. Of course, for a student of this style, the serial system can (and initially, probably should) be deterministic. But consider the great American saxophonist Charlie Parker's comment on the importance of learning the rules of harmony for improvisation, to the effect that the rules must be learned so that they can be forgotten.

sculpture. But again, such a list could continue indefinitely; the point is that we do, as perceivers and interpreters, participate in a critical enterprise that like the learning of a specific language with its comprehended aims and functions, allows us to distinguish between the master and the novice, between the coherent and the unintelligible, between the inventive and the formulaic, between the insightful and the commonplace, between the justifiable expansion of the stylistic range and the utterly incongruous. We are also able to distinguish between the meaningful and the vacuous, the significant and the empty. But this, in connection with language-games, we must look into more closely.

Wittgenstein identified the superfluity of Frege's attempt to display the nature of assertion by inserting "It is asserted:" before the propositional claim that "such-and-such is the case." It appears that we are often quick to recognize analogous superfluity or emptiness in visual or musical form. In some Spanish architectural decoration, for example, one sees the repetition of the visual theme to the point of exhausting redundancy.[25] One wants to say here, where indeed this expression is itself further evidence of our seeing within the context of a visual language-game[26] that "the same thing is being said over and over." As we know, that we are inclined to put the matter this way need not commit us to try to describe what it is that is being said outside the work in question[27]—this would indeed

---

25. See Roger Scruton's discussion of the Spanish Baroque or "Churrigueresque" style in the Charterhouse at Granada, in *The Aesthetics of Architecture* (Princeton: Princeton University Press, 1979), p. 208.

26. For an elucidation of the notion of seeing within a now-remote context, and its significance for art-historical methodology, see Michael Baxandall, "The Period Eye," in *Painting and Experience in Fifteenth-Century Italy* (Oxford: Oxford University Press, 1972).

27. On the ill-motivated desire to describe what it is that is "being said" in a work *outside* of any reference to the work in question, see my "Creation as Translation," *Journal of Aesthetics and Art Criticism* 46 (Winter 1987): 249–58.

be to transgress the limits of the game. In the same way, many critics of the musical direction known as minimalism criticize it for its redundancy; it too seems to say the same thing over and over. Its defenders, of course, are quick to observe that this is indeed the point, where a single thematic gesture is made, itself suggesting the melodic and rhythmic context—the intrinsic range of melodic, harmonic, and rhythmic permutational possibilities, within which that single gesture will be very gradually transformed. In short, the defense of auditory minimalism is that this musical language is a microcosm within which we become acutely aware of incremental expansion, where the sense of each transformation is guaranteed by its thematic progenitor. This debate, as it has developed, is a debate about a stylistic language-game.

We also saw, in Wittgenstein's elucidation of the idea of a language-game, how the limits of the sayable are determined not by the imposition of some kind of external linguistic constraint or boundary but by the intrinsic reach of the collective possible moves within the game. Thus in the same way that the limits of one's visual field are not described by extrinsic demarcation from beyond that field,[28] but rather by its intrinsic reach, so the limits of the expressible within a language-game are in a sense self-determined or autonomous. I believe this is one of the few junctures between art and language where this view is more widely presumed (if unarticulated) in the arts than it is subscribed to as a view describing language. Indeed, the entire range of critical discourse concerned with the depth or, by contrast, the shallowness, of a given genre or style relies on

---

28. See Ludwig Wittgenstein, *Tractatus Logico-Philosophicus*, trans. D. F. Pears and B. F. McGuinness (London: Routledge & Kegan Paul, 1961). 5.6–5.641, and Peter Winch's discussion "Text and Context" in *Trying to Make Sense* (Oxford: Basil Blackwell, 1987), esp. pp. 22–26, in which Winch pursues the comparison between (1) the eye itself not being a "part of the visual field" and (2) the knowing subject's relation to the world that is known.

it. This would, of course, have to be argued through particulars, and once again the list could be long. But a few cases here too will suffice to point the direction.

One might say of Vivaldi that although his instrumental music is pleasant, it is rarely deep; the range of expression within that harmonic vocabulary is intrinsically delimited in a way that precludes depth. Thus the criticism is not in this case that *Vivaldi* failed, for he most assuredly, as a master *of that style*, did not. If pressed, the same critic may elaborate by placing a contrasting case next to it, saying that although Bartok's *Concerto for Orchestra* is rarely pleasant, it is always deep. A critic might object to the inclusion of Norman Rockwell on a list of important American painters, saying that the interest is with *artists*, not craftsmen. That is, the moves of a very narrow (and in this case, naively sentimental) game are deployed over and over again, with no thought of expansion. If challenged here, that critic might point to Picasso's "Blue" period, which is admittedly sentimental, and in a respect naively so, but which is also something Picasso transcended. That early style and its intrinsic limits gave way to many later (and better) ones. Unlike Rockwell, this argument would proceed, Picasso did not fall victim to craftsmanly complacency. And indeed, to criticize an artist for being "trapped" in a narrow style is to register a desire for that artist to locate and begin work on sites for expansion. In a similar fashion, to claim that a style is now exhausted is to claim that all the moves housed within it have become excessively familiar and hence that inside *this* game it is now impossible to "say" anything new. This was in fact said of serial music a number of times, and each time another parameter was brought into the serial vocabulary thus expanding the limits of that language. Artists can also express the feeling that although a language may not have been exhausted in the preceding sense, a master of that language has made contributions within it and has seen nonobvious moves and made them, in a way beyond the capacity of the artist in question. This feeling is often musically expressed by jazz musicians playing in the modern style by "quoting" (itself a revealing locution) a passage of Charlie Parker's at a difficult point in the harmonic terrain, thus acknowledging the depth and insight of Parker's move at that juncture. This brief list of examples can extend into architecture in controversial cases such as the addition to Frank Lloyd Wright's Guggenheim Museum and whether or not it is perfectly consonant with the visual language of the main structure. This case involves disputes over both the appropriateness of the expansion of a stylistic language and the resultant juxtaposition of stylistically incongruous buildings behind the addition; whether, in short, those language-games are compatible such that a point of convergence can be found. An even more vociferous debate arose over Michael Graves's proposed additions to the Whitney Museum in New York. In the early design, the original structure was consumed within Graves's new postmodern full-block facade. The existing, original, internally-consistent facade was to be subsumed entirely into Graves's own visual language; in a more recent and moderate plan the stylistic consistency, and initial autonomy, of the original structure has been acknowledged. In these cases, we encounter strenuous debates concerning depth, quality, justifiability, appropriateness, redundancy, content, and so on through broad stretches of our critical vocabularies. And the internal logic of these aesthetic debates mirrors the characteristics of language-games identified by Wittgenstein.

In my opening remarks on language-games as employed by Wittgenstein in the philosophy of language, I said that only at the end of the discussion would it be possible to address the question of whether or not "language-games" would prove to be trivial exercises, or in the final analysis "only a game." Whatever the ultimate answer to that question, it seems clear that if employing the language-game strategy within aesthetics can yield at least provisional insight into problems of artistic coherence, expansion, invention, expressive limits, intelligibility, mastery, exhaustion, depth, stylistic integrity, the cohesion of materials and the like, and if it can lend at least some clarity to our view of how artistic meaning arises within contexts and remind us of the multiplicity of artistic meanings—or aims, functions, and uses—then the value of the language-game strategy seems assured; some mist enshrouding the concept of artistic meaning has been cleared. And if further consideration of the characteristics of a language-game leads to an awareness of the perfectly analogous characteristics of an artistic style, then to pursue the larger analogy between language and art is by no means just a game. Also, of course, to remove the central impediment to the "clear vision" of language Wittgenstein initially spoke of, that is, the "general notion of the meaning of a word," is also to remove the analogical basis for the general notion of the meaning of a work of art. And concerning limits, it was in his early philosophy, in which a concern with linguistic limits was nearer the surface of the text, that Wittgenstein said, "The limits of *language*... mean the limits of *my* world."[29] Even if we now know that the limits are, from the very nature of the diverse phenomena under investigation, perennially in flux, if we have reason to accept the appropriation of language-games to artistic styles, we might say with some accuracy that the systematically fluctuating limits of stylistic language-games are, taken *in toto*, the limits of the art world. The varieties of meaning contained within those limits, however, are best illuminated not directly by the notion of language-games, but rather by the related—but different—notion of a form of life.

29. *Tractatus Logico-Philosophicus*, 5.62.

2

～ Forms of Life and Artistic Practices

If it is true, as Wittgenstein puts it in his most succinct formulation of this point, that "to imagine a language means to imagine a form of life," and if it is also true that art is in at least some sense a language, then it would be difficult to avoid the conclusion that to imagine an art form means to imagine a form of life.[1] But before hastening toward any such conclusion, and certainly before knowing what such a conclusion in fact means, we must first explore what Wittgenstein meant by the phrase "form of life," and moreover what it means to *imagine* a language. Any incremental understanding gained on this matter holds unquestionable value for its power to cast light both on the analogy between art and language and on the issues surrounding the phrase "a form of life." Too often these issues are only vaguely attached to the phrase, but their importance to aesthetics is quite clear, for they include such matters as the significance of rituals to thought and feeling, the primitive and instinctive foundations of language, the point at which explanations come to an end, the notion of the mastering of a tech-

---

1. Ludwig Wittgenstein, *Philosophical Investigations*, 3d ed., trans. G. E. M. Anscombe (New York: Macmillan, 1952), sec. 19. The definitive succinct statement of this position is found in Richard Wollheim, *Art and Its Objects*, 2d ed. (Cambridge: Cambridge University Press, 1980), sec. 45–58.

nique, the immediate expression of emotion within human contexts, and the larger idea of a linguistic community.

The Concept of a Form of Life

Immediately preceding the claim that to imagine a language is to imagine a form of life, Wittgenstein says, "It is easy to imagine a language consisting only of orders and reports in battle.—Or a language consisting only of questions and expressions for answering yes and no. And innumerable others" (*Philosophical Investigations*,, sec. 19). This passage clearly connects the notion of a form of life to that of a language-game, but in a sense it does so too well, for it has suggested to some that they are interchangeable, and thus at least roughly equivalent. They are not. Wittgenstein does reinforce the connection between these two notions, but he also provides good reason for doubting their identity: "Here the term 'language-game' is meant to bring into prominence the fact that the *speaking* of language is part of an activity, or of a form of life" (*PI*, sec. 23). Thus we might well think of a language-game in which the outer expressive limits are marked by a small set of questions and the answers "yes" and "no," or another in which *only* battle-orders and reports are exchanged, so that to think beyond this range of expression, from within this game, would be to try to give propositional form to the ineffable. We are thus in possession of a rough idea of what it is to imagine a language-*game* (but not yet, to be sure, a *language*), and we are also similarly in a position to see that to imagine a language-game requires a set of roots reaching down into human action and practices.[2] Speaking is, indeed, an instance of, or part of,

---

2. See Renford Bambrough, "The Roots of Moral Reason," in *Gewirth's Ethical Rationalism*, ed. Edward Regis, Jr. (Chicago: University of Chicago Press, 1984); I am also here indebted to his lecture "The Roots of Critical Reason,"

activity; what Wittgenstein opposes here is the view that language does float freely, without roots to action and practice, "above" the world to which it refers. A language-game, then, is, as it involves speaking, a part of an activity; and as an activity it is *part* of—but not wholly identical with—a form of life.

We find another piece of the puzzle in the next appearance of the phrase, specifically in the erroneous ways of the interlocutor. The interlocutor, always quick to think within the confines of traditional philosophical categories, asks, "So you are saying that human agreement decides what is true and what is false?" (*PI*, sec. 241). That is to say, is it not true, with words on one side and the world on the other, that truth is *merely* a function of the agreements implicitly resident within our language? This naive-conventionalist account is as quickly not denied but rather repudiated by Wittgenstein: "It is what human beings *say* that is true and false; and they agree in the *language* they use." That is to say, as words are deeds,[3] and as we have already seen that to speak is to act and moreover that no action is independent of or outside a context (the notion of context-free speech is self-evidently absurd), then agreement, and truth, *could* not hover above the world, uprooted from human practices or human *language*. Thus, Wittgenstein adds, "That is not agreement in opinions but in form of life." Like the language within which it is manifest, human agreement is not, in opposition to naive linguistic conventionalism,[4] superficial. And in a quite different epistemological discussion, concerned with the function of doubt and what might be called the phe-

---

delivered at Cambridge University as part of the lecture series "Cambridge English" organized by George Watson, March 6, 1989.

3. For a related discussion, see Peter Winch, *"Im Anfang war die Tat,"* in *Trying to Make Sense* (Oxford: Basil Blackwell, 1987).

4. By "naive" I refer here to the presumption that words are arbitrary signs attached by convention to their otherwise disassociated meanings; I discuss this view in connection with aesthetics my "Language of Feeling," *The Journal of Comparative Literature and Aesthetics* (forthcoming).

nomenology of knowing,[5] Wittgenstein remarks, "Now I would like to regard this certainty, not as something akin to hastiness or superficiality, but as a form of life."[6] And reflecting on what he has just said, as a way of further exposing its roots to human or lived practices, he adds, "But that [the previous remark] means I want to conceive it as something that lies beyond being justified or unjustified; as it were, as something animal."[7] "Something animal" is not, presumably, going to float in a sphere of abstracted reflection and arbitrary agreement above and beyond the context of experience. And the next appearance of the phrase in *Philosophical Investigations* occurs at the opening of part II, in which we find a discussion of the mental life of, indeed, a dog.

Pursuing the question of why we can well imagine a dog frightened or startled but not hopeful,[8] Wittgenstein gives us the example "A dog believes his master is at the door" (*PI*, p. 174). So far, so good, but this is immediately followed by the question "But can he also believe his master will come the day after tomorrow?" To say that the dog believes his master is at the door does seem unproblematic; this might occur where the dog, say, hears the sounds of an approaching person and shows all the signs of canine excitement, but in fact we know his belief is unfounded; it is the postman. Of course when we say this of the dog, as we might to explain his excited behavior to someone in the room, we don't mean that the dog formulated a proposition and corroborated it by inquiring into states of affairs in the world. Beliefs, the attribution of belief, the excitation of

---

5. I am not suggesting here that Wittgenstein is any kind of phenomenologist; this way of putting the matter simply seems properly to underscore the shift of focus from objective states of external affairs to the *experience* of certainty.

6. *On Certainty* (Oxford: Basil Blackwell, 1969), sec. 358.

7. Ibid., sec. 359.

8. Naturally Wittgenstein is interested in revealing something about the logic of the employment of the concept of hope, not about canine phenomenology.

the dog, and our recognition of the dog's mistake do not in this way sever words from the world—or language from a form of life. But when we proceed to the next question, that is, whether or not the dog holds a capacity to believe its master will come in two days, we sense incoherence and find ourselves puzzled about how precisely to proceed. Thus Wittgenstein asks, "And *what* can he not do here?" where the "what" registers the frustration one feels at not knowing even how to begin to characterize the thing the dog *cannot* do. It is not that this particular dog cannot perform a certain feat, a feat within the capacities of some dogs but not this one, for example, jumping through a hoop. It is rather that the question insistently forces us to transgress the limits of the language-game, or, as we might now begin to see, to ask a question that does not have roots extending into known practice. Wittgenstein proceeds, leading us into the issue of mastering a technique: he asks, "Can only those hope who can talk?" And quickly answers, "Only those who have mastered the use of a language." That is, a *language* in the sense that Wittgenstein gives the term, not as it is understood in conventionalist theories of language. Such a (Wittgensteinian) language is rooted in a complex web of human practices where the employments of words themselves constitute some of those practices and itself engenders the mental and emotional phenomena of hoping. This formulation gives new application to and thus revives the claim made in the *Tractatus Logico-Philosophicus*:"The limits of *language*... mean the limits of *my* world."[9] When that claim was first made, Wittgenstein meant something utterly different by "language." Now, in the late works, "language" must be understood instrumentally, connected with language-games, and, most important, as inextricably rooted in deeds. Thus Wittgenstein says, "Only those [can hope] who have mastered the use of a language"

---

9. Ludwig Wittgenstin, *Tractatus Logico-Philosophicus*, trans. D. F. Pears and B. F. McGuinness (London: Routledge & Kegan Paul, 1961), 5.62.

because "the phenomena of hope are modes of this complicated form of life."

The final appearance of the phrase "form of life" in *Philosophical Investigations* marks a point of convergence with multiple resonances. The nature of certainty, the limits of epistemological doubt, and the end of explanation are all present in the claim "What has to be accepted, the given, is—so one could say—*forms of life*" (*PI*, p. 226). We shall return to the more focused significance of the resonances; for the present we must look into the theme that this remark makes most salient, the immediacy, or specifically the nonmediated or unconsidered character of forms of life, and to pursue this matter we must look into the logic of gesture.

In his early comments on Sir James George Frazer's *Golden Bough*,[10] Wittgenstein says, "We have in the ancient rites the use of a very highly developed gesture-language." With this remark he links the culturally deep practices of ritual with the concept of language by introducing the notion of a gesture language. Such a language of gestures might well constitute the paradigm case of a nonverbal language-game; that is, a set of moves embedded within a set of social practices that carry meaning—and in the case of rites, deep meaning—that nevertheless defy verbal or propositional formulation. It is true that the phrase "nonverbal language-game" seems self-contradictory at best, but if we recall gestures *do* carry meaning, and that they often speak louder than the accompanying words, which might well be incompatible with them, the phrase is not as self-contradictory as it seems. Moreover, if gesture at its best or highest,[11] that is, ritual, possesses meaning *like* language but

---

10. Rush Rhees, "Wittgenstein on Language and Ritual," in *Wittgenstein and His Times*, ed. Brian McGuinness (Oxford: Blackwell, 1982), p. 69.

11. This is *not* to say that it follows from *respect* for a ritual that it is thereby morally acceptable or that it should continue despite all costs and relevant particular considerations for evaluating it. See Richard Wollheim, *The Sheep*

not *within* language, then we are indeed approaching a very promising analogy for the understanding of art.

In a remark in the *Philosophical Investigations* made in connection with the larger discussion of the perception of an agent's following of a rule Wittgenstein makes it clear that he sees the capacity for meaning in gesture as an illuminating aspect of linguistic meaning: "Suppose you came as an explorer into an unknown country with a language quite strange to you. In what circumstances would you say that the people there gave orders, understood them, obeyed them, rebelled against them, and so on?" (sec. 206). These actions are, of course, various individual moves available within this heretofore unknown language-game; and although they are individual moves (to give an order is not to rebel against it), they intersect within the practices of the people of this unknown country in such a way that an autonomous move, for example, giving an order without the interrelated *possibility* of its being understood, is inconceivable. Wittgenstein makes it plain on the next line that gesture, broadly speaking, as it occurs within that witnessed set of practices, is fundamental to our coming to understand those practices: "The common behavior of mankind is the system of reference by means of which we interpret an unknown language." That Wittgenstein links speech to gesture and not to abstract logic is reinforced in further remarks in the early manuscript on Frazer,[12] in which he says, "Understanding negation is seeing the defensive gesture in it... understanding negation is the same as understanding a defensive gesture."[13]

This association of linguistic meaning with gestural

---

and the Ceremony, Leslie Stephen Lecture 1979 (Cambridge: Cambridge University Press, 1979), esp. pp. 26–33.

12. This is reported by Rush Rhees in "Wittgenstein on Language and Ritual"; in what follows I am much indebted to both his discussion of this topic and his insightful placement of relevant passages and quotations.

13. Rhees, "Wittgenstein on Language and Ritual," p. 71.

meaning[14] not only emphasizes the roots of meaning as they run through human practices and contexts but also "depsychologizes" meaning: that is, gestural meaning made salient discourages linguistic mentalism. In art, liberation from the aesthetic analogue to mentalism can prove clarifying on a range of artistic topics from creation to criticism. But before progressing beyond the topic of gesture in connection with the project of assembling a comprehension of the phrase "a form of life," we should glance at a few examples. Commonplace examples show the mutual reliance of the verbal and the gestural: "Shrugs, shakes of the head, nods, etc. are called signs principally because they are embedded in the way we use our spoken language."[15] Concerning ritual, Rush Rhees says:

> The ritual *means* something to those who celebrate or take part in it. Depending on which rite it is, there must be just these gestures, just these words must be uttered, and they must come in this order. What is done and spoken in the ritual refers to something important in the lives of the people who practice it: to sunrise at the solstices or equinoxes, to planting and harvesting, to the coming of the rainy season, to birth, to marriage, to burial, to going into battle, etc. It can do this, it has this significance because "it is the same language"—the language in which they plan and go about their sowing and harvesting, the language of their hopes and fears regarding it.[16]

Here it is clear that the particular actions of the ritual as properly performed, as deeds, are meaningful through their

---

14. See Norman Malcolm's discussion of a Neopolitan gesture indicating contempt performed by Piero Sraffa and directed to Wittgenstein accompanied by the query "What is the logical form of *that?*" which Malcolm suggests "broke the hold on him of the conception that a proposition must literally be a 'picture' of the reality it describes," in *Ludwig Wittgenstein: A Memoir*, with a biographical sketch by G. H. Von Wright (Oxford: Oxford University Press, 1958), p. 69.

15. *MS* 116, 262; quoted in Rhees, "Wittgenstein on Language and Ritual," pp. 71–72.

16. Rhees, "Wittgenstein on Language and Ritual," p. 72.

connection with the hopes and fears of the participants. Rhees mentions a curiously powerful example of such a ritualistic practice (discussed by Wittgenstein from *The Golden Bough*), the "ceremony of adopting a child, in which the mother draws the child through her clothes."[17] Rhees says of this case that it "is like a figure of speech; something like a *description* of actual birth, although a symbolic and abbreviated one. It is a figure which *might* have been used to tell of an actual birth; but this is not how it is in the ceremony. She is not describing what has happened or trying to tell anyone what it is like."[18] Indeed, the gesture, seen from the right perspective, possesses a remarkable power and is, if anything is, laden with meaning. Yet, for all that implicit significance, it is *not* a form of putting forward a proposition, of making an assertion, of giving a description. This is a human practice, although like language in its richness of meaning, far deeper than that of merely telling. As a ritualistic action it possesses a meaning with roots running through hopes and fear, through thoughts and feelings, and is thus very much like *language*; it is not at all like a propositional theory of language.

Within the philosophy of language, however, we might well ask, if the analogy between language and art is to prove ultimately illuminating, have we been given a new candidate for the essence of language and linguistic meaning? Have we, indeed, encountered a claim, in some way still inexact, that *gesture*, where this is thought to be rooted in practice and an unmediated form of expression, is the essence of linguistic meaning? The answer, of course, is clearly negative. In *Philosophical Investigations*, section 92, Wittgenstein writes, "This finds expression in questions as to the *essence* of language, of propositions, of thought—For if we too in these investigations are trying to understand the essence of language—its function, its struc-

---

17. Ibid., p. 73.
18. Ibid.

ture.—yet *this* is not what those questions have in view. For they see in the essence, not something that already lies open to view and that becomes surveyable by a rearrangement, but something that lies *beneath* the surface. Something that lies within, which we see when we look *into* the thing, and which an analysis digs out."[19] To make the gestural power of language visible, and to do this by "rearranging" our philosophical expectations by bringing gesture and language into conceptual proximity and by showing the roots that gesture and ritual have in human practices and their resonances with thought and feeling, is precisely what the remarks on Frazer and investigations into gesture accomplish. But to go on to claim that gesture is, or may be, linguistic essence, is to succumb to conceptual relapse. This is indicated in Wittgenstein's next line " *'The essence is hidden from us'*: This is the form our problem now assumes." And analogously, in aesthetics, we would, succumbing to the same temptation, search for the *hidden essence* of artistic meaning. Going on, he adds, "We ask: *'What is* language?', *'What is* a proposition?' And the answer to these questions is to be given once for all; and independently of any future experience." In aesthetics, we would ask, "*What is* art?" "*What is* artistic meaning?" as though an answer could be provided not only in isolation from the artistic practices and contexts within which aesthetic gestures are significant but in isolation from, and prior to, any future experience of new artistic developments. Connecting language with gesture makes a number of features of language salient, features we would forget to our conceptual peril, but it does not make gesture linguistic essence. Still, to return to the example of the adoption rite, one might say that it *is* meaning-laden and that we want to know what it means apart from the description of the practice itself and its felt power. But this would be to insist that gestural meaning is, in

---

19. For a sustained discussion of Wittgenstein's own criticisms of the earlier view, see Norman Malcolm, *Nothing Is Hidden* (Oxford: Basil Blackwell, 1986).

the end, propositional. As Wittgenstein remarks in one of his manuscripts, "It is a great temptation, to try to make the spirit of something explicit."[20]

To attempt to render the spirit of the adoption rite explicit would be to see it as a function of some prior reasoning about its significance. In a discussion of the nature of certainty, Wittgenstein says, "I want to regard man here as an animal; as a primitive being to which one grants instinct but not ratiocination. As a creature in a primitive state."[21] Such a creature would engage in practices that embody certainty but do not follow from reflection about the certainty they implicitly embody. Perhaps "instinct" is the proper name for such practices; the "primitive being" acts within a context, within a language-game, in which words and deeds are not ontologically distinct and in which the significance of those words and deeds, the range of which is circumscribed by the limits of the game, is not the result of epistemological reflection and the rational overcoming of doubt. Does such a primitive picture, itself suggested as a corrective to the more familiar, overly intellectual one, in its turn oversimplify the logic of language? Wittgenstein continues the above passage with "Any logic good enough for a primitive means of communication needs no apology from us." And, summarizing the point of these remarks, he adds "Language did not emerge from some kind of ratiocination."[22] Thus the conception, the overview,[23] of situated language that emerges from the pursuit of the meaning of the phrase "a form of life" is startlingly unlike the conceptions of language that have been

20. Quoted in Rhees, "Wittgenstein on Language and Ritual," p. 93.
21. *On Certainty*, sec. 475.
22. See also *On Certainty*, sec. 477: "For why should the language game rest on some kind of knowledge?" Again, it is not prior thought that the moves in the game require for their sense. For the idea that language *needs* no foundation and that such a foundation would not in any case be what we expect it to be, see Wittgenstein, *Philosophical Investigations*, secs. 124 and 129.
23. By "overview" I mean one of the positive results of a philosophical investigation; I discuss this at greater length in the final section of Chapter 5.

traditionally influential in aesthetic theory; one can make this difference all the more explicit through the analogy between art and language by simply restating this claim: art did not emerge from some kind of ratiocination.[24] But again, at this point we are still building another basis for the multifaceted analogy between art and language on the linguistic side of the equation; the parallel discussion of art and literature is yet to come. For the present, in the interest of further establishing the basis for the analogy, we must look further into the nature of the "spirit" that it is tempting to try to make explicit.

According to Rhees, in his second set of comments on Frazer's *Golden Bough* Wittgenstein could have expressed his point well by saying that Frazer, although perfectly capable of giving detailed accounts of the history and precise practices of the fire festivals, did not grasp the spirit, the *Geist*, of those ritualistic practices.[25] Frazer's methodology committed him to grouping all the fire festivals of Europe together in one category. Of this search for commonality Wittgenstein commented, as Rhees reports, using the analogy of facial resemblance: "It is a wide variety of faces with common features... And one would like to draw lines joining the parts that various faces have in common. But then a part of our contemplation would still be lacking, and it is what connects this picture with our own feelings and thoughts. This part gives the contemplation its depth." Indeed, what the "picture" of the ritual presents, as that picture

---

24. Wittgenstein clearly meant this claim (as applied to language) as a corrective; the line of thought cannot be taken too far, as it is, for example, in the erroneous claim that *all* language replaces natural emotional expression, or (as applied to art) in the equally erroneous claim that *all* art is a replacement for natural emotive behavior. A more accurate way of setting out the art-language analogy at this juncture is to say that just as language did not emerge from ratiocination, art did not emerge from thought about the possible combinations and interactions of arbitrary signifiers.

25. Rhees, "Wittgenstein on Language and Ritual," pp. 93–97. See also Frank Cioffi, "Wittgenstein and the Fire-Festivals," in *Perspectives on the Philosophy of Wittgenstein*, ed. Irving Block (Oxford: Basil Blackwell, 1981).

Forms of Life and Artistic Practices 57

is formed by tracing resemblances, is just what they have in common. And this strategy promises an understanding of the practices of precisely the sort that Frazer delivered, but systematically omits the connection to our feelings and thoughts, and thus fails to capture the spirit, the resonance, and the depth of the ritualistic practices. There is an all-too-common art-historical methodology analogous to Frazer's study of ritual. This "positivistic" approach documents and verifies the technical details of the history of a work of art in terms of commodity exchange. Like Frazer's, such an approach misses that vital connection to thought and feeling. Still, what *can* be said of this connection?[26]

Further into the discussion of ritual, Wittgenstein asks what it is that makes human sacrifice seem deeply sinister. He considers and rejects the hypothesis that this sinister effect is a direct function of the suffering and loss of the victim: "All manner of diseases bring just as much suffering and do *not* make this impression."[27] Apparently recalling the shortcomings of Frazer's account and reflecting on how very much the method of searching for external features common to many different ritualistic practices misses, he adds, "No, this deep and sinister aspect is not obvious just from learning the history of the external action, but *we* impute it from an experience in ourselves." In commenting on these remarks of Wittgenstein's, Rhees directs our attention to the particular expressions Wittgenstein employs which include the phrase "that which I see in those stories"[28] and the phrase above, "this deep and sinister aspect." At a glance one can see here the clear connection with Wittgenstein's discussion of aspect perception and "seeing-as" (*PI*, part II, sec. xi). And within this glance one issue is vividly clear:

---

26. For an analysis of the parallel between the correspondence of (1) emotion with a natural scene and (2) emotion with a work of art, i.e., the connection of thought with feeling, see Wollheim, *The Sheep and the Ceremony*.
27. Rhees, "Wittgenstein on Language and Ritual," p. 100.
28. Ibid.

a central theme of the remarks on aspect perception is that it is not possible to distinguish the "given" in visual experience (seeing) from the "interpretation" (or thinking) of that experience. Instead, the perception of an aspect of a thing seems to suffuse the perceived object with the thought. Rhees makes the crucial connection here between Wittgenstein's thoughts on ritual and on aspect perception by quoting the now well-known passage, "But what I perceive in the dawning of an aspect is not a property of the object, but an internal relation between it and other objects."[29] And what was missed, in Frazer's account, was the "spirit", that is, the connections between our thoughts and feelings and the ritual. This spirit, which gives a ritual its depth, is nothing other than the indivisible perception of the thoughts and feelings *in* that ritual. And in a perfectly analogous way, what gives the later works of Rothko, for example, their curiously engaging depth are precisely the thoughts and feelings we perceive in them. Thus it is not the outward, physicalistic description of a work of art that can account for its depth, its engaging quality, or the ideas, thoughts, feelings, social practices,[30] or precedents that we find in it. It is, rather—and to this topic we shall have occasion to return in connection with literary interpretation—its spirit.

Wittgenstein said of the ancient rites that they comprise a "very highly developed gesture-language" and that the "ritual of the ancient myths was a language."[31] We have seen that an

---

29. Ibid., p. 102.

30. See Wittgenstein's remark, quoted in Rhees, "Wittgenstein on Language and Ritual," p. 106: "In all these practices we see something that is similar, at any rate, to the association of ideas and related to it. We could speak of an association of practices." For an example of one such association of practices in visual art, see Kirk Varnedoe's identification of the impulses motivating Picasso and Gaugin as primitive, in *A Fine Disregard: What Makes Modern Art Modern* (New York: Abrams, 1990), p. 185; see also Varnedoe's discussion of Aby Warburg's perception of the "root similarities" of European and primitive art, pp. 191–92.

31. Rhees, "Wittgenstein on Language and Ritual," p. 69.

investigation into the meanings of the phrase "a form of life" itself constitutes an investigation into Wittgenstein's later conception of language. And it is clear that it is this conception of language which will prove illuminating in art as the basis for the analogy—or multifarious analogies—between language and art. But before turning directly to the application of this conception of language to art the conception itself still has to be more fully elaborated. Before pursuing that elaboration, it is worth commenting on one further aspect of the phrase "a form of life." This phrase, after all, incorporates metaphorically the concept of *life*, and with this metaphorical description of language we ought not to be surprised if, as a result of the analogical connection of art with language, we encounter a description of the power a work of art, as a perfect analogue to a human being, has to connect its "spirit" to thoughts and feelings.

Gesture, Ritual, and Artistic "Spirit"

It is clear that the phrase "form of life" is meant, in part, to prevent dualistic mentalism from influencing the shaping of a conception of meaning. Late in part I of *Philosophical Investigations* Wittgenstein suggests that one might distinguish between "surface grammar" (*PI*, sec. 664) and "depth grammar" in the use of words, but qualifies this suggestion by adding that what "immediately impresses itself upon us about the use of a word is the way it is used in the construction of the sentence." Thus, to rephrase, a word is an utterance defined by its instrumental function in a specific context and *not* an arbitrary signifier set against the background of a sentence. Moreover, as should be clear from the preceding, this context is not the result of our perception, but, as a form of life, it is a given. Wittgenstein continues by adding that what immediately, as opposed to mediately, strikes us is "the part of its use—one might say—that can be taken in by the ear."

Having established the instrumental employment of a word within a given context, Wittgenstein moves on to repudiate the very notion of depth grammar, showing how this notion is conceptually disorienting: "And now compare the depth grammar, say of the word 'to mean', with what its surface grammar would lead us to suspect. No wonder we find it difficult to know our way about." That is, having first been given a clear view of functional meaning within an immediately grasped context, we then utterly obscure this newfound understanding with the metaphor of depth and imply the existence of an intangible and ultimately hidden realm of "meanings." It is no wonder, indeed, that we then feel haunted by meanings we can sense but not articulate. Nor is such a haunted condition unfamiliar to the practitioners of aesthetics who having implicitly subscribed to the mentalism Wittgenstein is undermining, define the central task of aesthetic theory as the development of a method for pursuing such meanings.[32] Does this emphasis on context thus imply that the meaning is on the surface? The answer to this question must be both yes and no: "yes" in the sense that the elucidation of the phrase "form of life" leads us to look at instrumental function within given contexts and not "beneath" them; "no" in the sense that the very distinction between surface and depth suggests that the operative concept of meaning as it is attached to surface-meaning and depth-meaning is acceptable, and that we must simply choose the former. But this conception is decidedly *not* acceptable, for reasons Wittgenstein makes clear in section 665: "Imagine

---

32. Much of the debate concerning the significance of intention for interpretation shares this mentalistic conception of the task of aesthetic theory; I discuss some cases in my "Artistic Intention and Mental Image," *Journal of Aesthetic Education* 22 (Fall 1988): 63–75. See also Colin Lyas, "Personal Qualities and the Intentional Fallacy," in *Philosophy and the Arts*, Royal Institute of Philosophy Lectures, vol. 6, ed. Godfrey Vesey (London: Macmillan, 1973).

someone pointing to his cheek with an expression of pain and saying 'abracadabra!'—we ask 'What do you mean?' and he answers 'I meant toothache'." This is indeed a perfect illustration of the shallowness of the mentalistic, conventional understanding of meaning as somehow hidden behind or beneath the arbitrary word or sign. Surely rightly, Wittgenstein says next, "You at once think to yourself: How can one 'mean toothache' by that word?"... Or what did it *mean* to *mean* pain by that word?" Indeed, not only is the notion of the hidden meaning obscure, but it is not clear whether we can mean anything *by* this conception of meaning. "And yet," he then adds as a reminder of how familiar this conception of hidden meaning is to the philosophy of language, "in a different context, you would have asserted that the mental activity of *meaning* such-and-such was just what was most important in using language."

The aesthetic parallel is eminently clear: when discussed in connection with a *particular* artistic gesture in a *particular* context and style, meaning is vividly apparent. By contrast, when discussed as the hidden product of private mental intention, meaning is, as the target of criticism, disorienting at its very best. "But," one wants to insist, "can't I say By 'abracadabra', I mean toothache?" Wittgenstein answers, naturally, "Of course I can," but quickly adds, "But this is a definition; not a description of what goes on in me when I utter the word." The analogous lesson for aesthetics is equally clear: if an artist or writer means something by a particular work, and if we, as critics of that work, want to recover that meaning, we will not find it by trying to hunt down a hypothetical act of "meaning" that took place as the work was created or "uttered," but rather by looking to the particulars of the context within which that "utterance" was made.

Much earlier in *Philosophical Investigations* Wittgenstein remarks that for "a large class of cases—though not for all—in which we employ the word 'meaning' it can be defined thus: the meaning of a word is its use in the language" (*PI*, sec. 43).

If to imagine a language is to imagine a form of life, and if art is in this respect like language, then, employing the word "use" broadly, the meaning of a work is its use within the form of life of the world of art.

Another aspect of Wittgenstein's later conception of language to which we must return Wittgenstein called the mastery of a technique. To the question of whether it would be possible for *one* man to obey a rule only *once* in his life, Wittgenstein answers, "It is not possible that there should have been only one occasion on which someone obeyed a rule. It is not possible that there should have been only one occasion on which a report was made, an order given or understood, and so on" (*PI*, sec. 199). Making this fact salient for the later, larger conception of language, he adds, "To obey a rule, to make a report, to give an order, to play a game of chess, are *customs* (uses, institutions)."[33] Thus meaning has a public character or dimension, which implies a concern for context. He continues, reiterating the necessity of context for comprehension, "To understand a sentence means to understand a language. To understand a language means to be a master of a technique." The first assertion emphasizes that a sentence is uttered, not in the solitary mental world of a private rule-follower, but within a linguistic *community*. The second emphasizes that sentences are instrumental, and thus that a sentence is uttered in *practice*. He takes up this conception of unmediated and uninterpreted practice in following sections.

Wittgenstein identifies, in section 201 of *Philosophical Inves-*

---

33. The attempt to define art as whatever an institution of some sort calls art does not, of course, constitute a development of this point; that obeying a rule, making a report, giving an order, and playing chess are, in this sense, customs, uses, and institutions, does not mean that an essence is given to these activities by their "institutional" contexts. Moreover, even if such a classification were established the reasons or justifications for it would nevertheless remain utterly unexplained. See Richard Wollheim, "The Institutional Theory of Art," Supplementary Essay 1, in *Art and Its Objects*, pp. 157–66.

tigations, within his larger discussion of rule-following, what has been referred to as a skeptical problem,[34] that is, that we face a paradox in the realization that no action could be determined by a rule, "because every course of action can be made out to accord with the rule." And, conversely, if every course can be made to fit the rule then it can equally be made discordant with the rule. "And so there would be neither accord nor conflict here." So there is no determination of a particular action by a particular rule, because any action can be shown to be in accord with an infinite number of other rules; in short, no *one* rule can be designated as the determining rule for an action, and thus the accord/disaccord distinction loses its sense. But of this problem we see an objection to its very formulation quickly registered in the following remark pertaining to the infinite regression of interpretations of the rule as the rule variously determines its corresponding course of action:[35] "It can be seen that there is a misunderstanding here from the mere fact that in the course of our argument we give one interpretation after another; as if each one contented us at least for a moment, until we thought of yet another standing behind it." Thus each interpretation, as an act of ratiocination on the relation between the rule and its corresponding action, quickly yields to a competing interpretation of that relationship, which in turn gives way to another, *ad infinitum*. "What this shows is that there is a way of grasping a rule which is *not* an *interpretation*, but which is exhibited in what we call 'obeying the rule' and 'going against it' in actual cases." Interpretation is, again, ratiocination, and

---

34. This skeptical Humean light on the issue is cast in Saul Kripke, *Wittgenstein on Rules and Private Language* (Oxford: Basil Blackwell, 1982); the argument that this way of putting the matter is alien to Wittgenstein's enterprise is found in G. P. Baker and P.M.S. Hacker, *Scepticism, Rules and Language* (Oxford: Basil Blackwell, 1984), esp. chapter 1, "On Misunderstanding Wittgenstein: Kripke's Private Language Argument," pp. 1–55.

35. This objection to the very formulation of the problem is one of the considerations the Humean construal appears to undervalue.

as such exemplifies the very mentalism and psychologism that Wittgenstein opposes with his later conception of meaning. Hence, "there is an inclination to say: every action according to the rule is an interpretation." Simply put, if this is true, thought directs every action by providing a rule to govern that action. But according to Wittgenstein, "we ought to restrict the term 'interpretation' to the substitution of one expression of the rule for another." In this latter case, of course, thought *is* present behind action, although not in the way the mentalistic picture suggests. The thought is about the rule, normally obeyed or disobeyed in practice. Thus, the rule, not the action, is the actual subject of reflection, and is, when made manifest, an interpretation of the action rather than its governor. Thus following a rule is, in Wittgenstein's sense, participation in a form of life, or as Wittgenstein puts it in the opening remark of section 202, "And hence also 'obeying a rule' is a practice."

The aesthetic parallel to these linguistic considerations is surprisingly apparent if one looks in the right place, and this too further corroborates the conception of the world of art, through the analogy with Wittgenstein's later conception of language, as a form of life. Questions of rule-following are perhaps most accessible in musical composition. When Haydn or Mozart wrote a terminal cadence, that is, a harmonic conclusion in which the unresolved dominant comes to rest on the tonic, did they, as compositional ratiocination determining the course of harmonic action, say to themselves, "The dominant needs an internal tritone" or "The final tonic needs a prominent major third"? Surely not; only beginners do that, yet the compositional practices of Haydn and Mozart most assuredly embody those rules.[36] Indeed, this is the musical analogue to

---

36. See *Philosophical Investigations*, sec. 224: "The word 'agreement' and the word 'rule' are *related* to one another, they are cousins." Here, one might say, Haydn and Mozart, through practice-embedded rules, agree. See my "Music and Imagination," *Philosophy* 61 (October 1986): 513–17, for specific examples. For an accurate treatment of the logically primitive nature of agreements in

Wittgenstein's remark in section 219: "When I obey a rule, I do not choose. I obey the rule *blindly*." In the case of Stravinsky, there is a recent interpretation of his entire *opus* suggesting that in fact there is a large-scale coherence running throughout

---

judgment, see Anthony Palmer, *Concept and Object* (London: Routledge, 1988), pp. 90–106. Of Wittgenstein's imagined book on anthropology, he said it "would begin by stressing the central role of a particular way in which human beings agree in what they say and do in any endeavour to understand them in their different societies." Palmer maintains that this book would make salient "that agreement which in the *Philosophical Investigations* is said to be necessary if language is to be a means of communication, necessary, that is, for there to be societies at all." Communication in art would, naturally, to the extent that it is language-like in its origins and functions, require parallel agreements for there to be artistic activity in society at all. Palmer makes it clear that it is a special variety of agreement under discussion here—one that stands before or beneath ratiocination. The immediately relevant passage from *Philosophical Investigations*, which Palmer discusses, is "If language is to be a means of communication there must be agreement not only in definition but also, queer as this may sound, in judgements. This seems to abolish logic but does not do so" (quoted in *Concept and Object*, p. 88).

It is certainly worth noting here as well that in his description of F. B. Ebersole's *Things We Know* (Eugene: University of Oregon Press, 1967), Palmer says that through the employment of "devastating examples [Ebersole shows] that the attempt to understand human behaviour by beginning with something which is not human behaviour, but, as the older psychologists used to say, 'mere bodily movements'... and interpreting them by setting them in a particular background is hopeless." Palmer then shows that "this was indeed, the way in which Strawson was constrained to think and speak about other people." As I have argued elsewhere, Joseph Margolis, through the explicit appropriation of the Strawsonian model, and Arthur Danto, through the atomism implicit in his theory and his reductive program reaching back to the "mere real thing," are similarly constrained to think of art in this way.

For helpful discussions of the value of examples for philosophical method, see R. W. Newell, *Objectivity, Empiricism, and Truth* (London: Routledge & Kegan Paul, 1986), esp. "Reason and Particular Cases: John Wisdom," pp. 85–100, and Onora O'Neill, "The Power of Example," *Philosophy* 61 (January 1986): 5–29. On the issue of ratiocination in connection with consciousness, self-understanding, and the location of meaning in a form of life instead of in the mind of a speaker, see the stimulating essays by Jonathan Lear, "On Reflection: The Legacy of Wittgenstein." *Ratio* 2 (June 1989): 19–45, and "Transcendental Anthropology," in Philip Pettit and John McDowell, *Subject, Thought, and Context*, ed. (Oxford: Clarendon Press, 1986).

his work, in that it depends for its harmonic generation on a heretofore undetected septatonic scale.[37] The point here is precisely that a new *interpretation* has been given, because in the restricted sense as suggested above, the governing rule behind the harmonic practice is *itself* the object of contemplation. In plainsong and early monody one could insist that the rule of, quite simply, harmonizing nothing, leaving only unaccompanied melodic movement, is followed consciously and rigorously. Of course, any rational person sensitive to the dangers of critical anachronism would strongly object to this construction; monody was a musical *practice* and as the "given" conception of the music of the period, although perhaps in retrospect in accord with, surely did not *follow* any such rule. Debussy, as is well known, was severely reprimanded by his instructors for failing to follow the rules of harmony, or, better, the rules of harmonic practice of late nineteenth-century Paris. What then are his parallel harmonies, which satisfied only, as he put it, the rule of his ear, if not instances of " 'going against [the rule]' in actual cases?" In visual cases, such as the jarring recognition of incorrect proportion in the classical orders, we see—and here is one of the many similarities between ethical and aesthetic perception—the rule only when it is broken, for most examples of the laws of classic proportion do not demand or even invite reflection on the rule itself. Similarly, we would experience a shock in reading the literary genre of magical realism *as* realism,[38] but the shock would subside as soon as we learned that realism of the magical variety does not accord with the temporal and ontological rules of realism; when we read each of these genres of fiction for what they are, the issue of rules sub-

---

37. See Pieter van den Toorn, *Stravinsky and the Rite of Spring: The Beginnings of a Musical Language* (Oxford: Oxford University Press, 1987).

38. I mean here the shock or severe confusion that would occur in trying to take, for example, Borges's cases of creating a person over time in an episodic dream or of repeatedly opening a book and each time finding different things in it, as realistic depictions of actual states of affairs.

merges—back into practice.[39] In all such cases, where we are following not labored and tenuous work but rather the work of the master of an art form—indeed the master of many techniques—the issue of rules, not subject to ratiocination, remains embedded within an artistic form of life.[40]

In a well-known passage meant to return the conception of rule-governed behavior from an infinitude of interpretations back to practice, Wittgenstein says, "If I have exhausted the justification, I have reached bedrock, and my spade is turned. Then I'm inclined to say: this is simply what I do" (*PI*, sec. 217).[41] This passage explicitly speaks to rule-following, but for that reason it is also significant for the understanding of interpretation, which is significant for the understanding of the directness of our perception of emotional expression and which is in turn significant for the understanding of our perception of emotional expression in art. Thus bringing us back into direct contact with the issue of facial expressivity, Wittgenstein introduces the topic "Consciousness in another's face," which he immediately follows with an example from actual practice: "Look into someone else's face, and see the consciousness in it, and a particular *shade* of consciousness. You see on it, in it, joy, indifference, interest, excitement, torpor, and so on."[42] These are, naturally, examples of an *uninterpreted* or unmediated perception of emotive and human qualities and experiences, and as such are familiar experiences situated within our form of life. As a way of making their uninterpreted perception clear,

---

39. In this connection, see also *Philosophical Investigations*, sec. 154: "If there has to be anything 'behind the utterance of the formula' it is *particular circumstances*."

40. A failure to recognize this embeddedness promotes the belief that every verbal utterance necessitates an interpretation of a linguistic rule, which in turn nourishes neo-Lockeian varieties of linguistic relativism.

41. See also *On Certainty*, secs. 97–99, for further discussion of the "bedrock" metaphor.

42. Ludwig Wittgenstein, *Zettel*, ed. G. E. M. Anscombe and G. H. von Wright, trans. G. E. M. Anscombe (Oxford: Basil Blackwell, 1967), sec. 220.

Wittgenstein asks, against their natural familiarity, "Do you look into *yourself* in order to recognize the fury in *his* face?" Against the background, the context, of familiarity he has just sketched, it is clear that any such introspection and analogical comparison would be extraordinarily unusual and, like the explicit consideration of rules, anything but the *basis* of the ordinary cases; indeed it is against the context of the ordinary cases that cases involving the explicit consideration of rules stand out. He then adds, as a parenthetical development of the philosophical view he is opposing and hence a further reminder of that view's capacity to generate nonsense, "And what do we want to say now? That someone else's face stimulates me to imitate it, and that I therefore feel little movements and muscle-contractions in my own face and *mean* the sum of these? Nonsense. Nonsense,—because you are making assumptions instead of simply describing. If your head is haunted by explanations here, you are neglecting to remind yourself of the most important facts." To be haunted by explanations, or by the demand for them,[43] here as before is to feel an illegitimate need for explanation beyond description. To develop this a bit further, Wittgenstein poses the case in which someone says to another, "I see the look that you cast at someone else." If the person spoken to were to claim that the speaker did "not really *see* it [Wittgenstein adds], I should take that for pure stupidity."[44] Of course, the statement that the speaker did "not really *see* it" isn't stupidity, because it is consistent with the dualistic view, in which meaning is inwardly determined and

---

43. See *Philosophical Investigations*, sec. 217: "(Remember that we sometimes demand definitions for the sake not of their content, but of their form. Our requirement is an architectural one; the definition of a kind of ornamental coping that supports nothing.)" An account of the demand in criticism for such "architectural" explanations of artistic meaning is given in my "Creation as Translation," *Journal of Aesthetics and Art Criticism* 46 (Winter 1987): 249–58.

44. *Zettel*, sec. 223.

emotional expression is encoded into physiognomy and decoded through analogical interpretation. It is, however, erroneous. The point is that according to the form-of-life conception of meaning, such acts of interpretation, in rule-following and in emotional perception, are conspicuously absent. Locating the aesthetic analogue to this discussion requires no searching; an entire world of art full of stylistically variegated depictions of human facial expressivity requires for its emotive impact no analogical imaginings of a diagnostic nature. This is, simply put, a matter of what we do not do, and in this connection Wittgenstein adds, "We do not see facial contortions and make inferences from them (like a doctor framing a diagnosis) to joy, grief, boredom. We describe a face immediately as sad, radiant, bored, even when we are unable to give any other descriptions of the features.—Grief, one would like to say, is personified in the face."[45] And, to make clear that these considerations are not merely reflections on what we happen to do or not in actual practice quite apart from any more philosophically elevated enterprise, Wittgenstein adds the pointed remark "This belongs to the concept of emotion." It is self-evident that the concept of emotion holds direct significance for our understanding of art, and it is to cases of such understandings that we should now turn.[46]

Meaning and Artistic Uses

Roughly fifteen thousand years ago a person painted a picture of a bison on a cave ceiling in what is now Altamira, Spain. Such paintings have given rise to a good deal of speculation. One hypothesis is that the making of a picture of a bison was

---

45. Ibid., sec. 225.
46. For a full discussion of the value of such a turn to cases, see O'Neill, "The Power of Example."

thought to yield a power over the living bison such that it could be killed; such a conception is obviously primitive and, indeed, what we might call magical. But for this primitive conception of magical causation, and of the power of mimetic depiction, it is a fascinating explanation, and the fascination lies not in a form of meaning hidden "beneath" the painting, but in the role visual representation—as we retrospectively call it—played in the lives of those cave dwellers. And of course, this explanation also makes clear that the power of depiction was *instrumental*; like voodoo practices,[47] it is the *making* of the depiction or the representation, and the ritualized acting on that depiction, that holds the power.

The introductory bassoon passage of Stravinsky's *Rite of Spring* is now widely misunderstood.[48] That its texture and its rhythmic ambiguities are aurally engaging, that they "grab the ear," as it is sometimes put, is obvious on the auditory "face" of the passage. But at the time Stravinsky wrote it, the extended upper range of the bassoon that is commonplace today was then unknown. As a result the original performance had a *very* tenuous and strained quality; indeed, anyone with a knowledge of the then-limited upper range would have listened, as we say, on the edge of the seat. The effect would have been roughly like that of hearing a mezzo-soprano take the soprano part and perform, although successfully, at the very limits of the possible. Knowing this transforms our perception of that introductory passage and allows us to hear it as a gesture at the limit of the expressive reach of the instrument.[49] And to understand that musical gesture properly is to see it in its initial context.

---

47. The similarity of function in these cases is mentioned by Susan Woodford, *Looking at Pictures* (Cambridge: Cambridge University Press, 1983), p. 7.

48. This case of instrumental range and the importance of original context for comprehending meaning was presented by Alexander Goehr in the lecture "Music and Communication" in the Darwin Lectures, Cambridge University, February 24, 1989.

49. I put it this way, i.e., hearing it *as* an instrumental gesture at the limits

In *Philosophical Investigations*, section 207, Wittgenstein remarks that it is the "common behavior of mankind" that serves as "the system of reference by means of which we interpret an unknown language." He continues, "Let us imagine that the people in that country carried on the usual human activities and in the course of them employed, apparently, an articulate language." On first hearing a performance of Elliott Carter's works for solo tympani, one finds oneself in an analogous position. It seems, at first, beyond intelligibility; then it seems to approximate coherence. Later, the performance seems to present an articulate language, and in the end one might well marvel at how articulate, throughout the expressive range and limits of the tympani, those works actually are. This process is not only aided by the context of the "common behavior" of musical coherence, which elicits our expectation of hearing, and our willingness to listen for such coherence, but also by "systems of reference" of rhythmic structure and repetition, pitch variation, and dynamic variation. And if we initially face, on first hearing those remarkable works, a question of meaning, it is a focused question asking for precisely this kind of progress toward intelligibility.

Within the context of Greek architecture the fact that there is a difference between Doric and Corinthian column capitals is of course significant. The Doric betokens purity and directness; the Corinthian, an increased concern for decoration and perhaps visual embellishment. And within this context, if one wanted to argue further for the distinction as it is here characterized, one could point to the other ends of the columns. The Doric stands directly on the stylobate; the more florid Corinthian meets a softening base before reaching the floor. These columns have been employed in a radically divergent context,

---

of its range because, of course, it no longer *is*; yet to hear it properly we must use our imaginations to hear it precisely in this way. In brief, knowledge of the context here transforms what we hear.

that of postmodern architecture, and in these uses of the Greek visual "utterances" there is, against the immediately preceding antihistorical modernism, a re-embracing of historical precedent. But the use of either the Doric or the Corinthian now carry that significance, in that both are certainly integrative gestures of our visual history and perhaps nostalgic in a self-conscious way. In the initial context, the difference between the two was crucial for their significance. In the present context, in which the additional meaning of historical eclecticism is now a possible move within the expanded stylistic game, they have similar meanings because they have very similar uses.

In Section 441 of *Philosophical Investigations*, Wittgenstein begins, "By nature and by particular training, a particular education, we are disposed to give spontaneous expression to wishes in certain circumstances," and a moment later adds, "In this game the question whether I know what I wish before my wish is fulfilled cannot arise at all." The context of modern jazz improvisation is a certain circumstance within which one gives spontaneous expression to musical ideas, where this capacity is a function of a particular training and education, but the question of whether or not the players know what they wish before the wish is fulfilled transgresses the limits of the game (the practices of an improvisational ensemble), because the dualistic scheme the question implies is not operative in the first place. It is, indeed, a question that cannot be answered, because its formulation is incoherent at worst, inapplicable to the case at best, and leads us to believe that the "meaning" of the improvisation must in a mysterious way lie behind the sonic surface in the private intentional world of the improvisers.

In Jackson Pollock's large action canvases we encounter visual surfaces that almost invariably provoke questions of meaning. This question is very often answered within the concept of "action" itself. These canvases are the visual analogue to a tape-recording of a concert; that is, they reveal what happened when they were created. And this in turn provokes, in further pursuit of meaning, the question of how they *were* made, and the processes of dripping, throwing, hurling, and so on are then described. It is in this connection that the frequent reproduction of the photograph of Pollock at work, standing over a canvas with brush and not palette but bucket in hand, is the visual answer to the question of meaning provoked by the canvases. (What other photographs of painters at work are in fact widely reproduced?) More considered questions of meaning lead to an inability, in Pollock's case, to distinguish between deliberation and execution, between form and content, between design and spontaneity, and between movement and stillness. And with titles such as "Autumn Rhythm," one might argue, in the continued inquiry into meaning, that the distinction between abstraction and representation has also been blurred. All of these considerations concern directly, immediately, and *unmysteriously*, the practices of an artist within the larger conceptual web, or aesthetic context, of these distinctions.

Roy Lichtenstein has produced a body of paintings that are generally construed as large-scale cartoons, with balloon-captions such as "I'd rather drown than call Brad for help...." But they are, of course, *not* large-scale cartoons, they are large-scaled detailed depictions of cartoons, and as such require the deliberate and exacting duplication of a number of features that are, at the relatively miniscule cartoon scale, accidental or inadvertent. For example, the stroke of a brush or a pen is, at a fine level, uneven; there are streaks and lines contained within the stroke that are functions not of deliberation but of the medium itself. Lichtenstein painstakingly duplicates such internally contained lines, and thus, through a dramatic change of scale, expands the "reach" of the intentional within the image; that is, he pulls the accidental visual features into the realm of the deliberate—and skilled—moves of the visual game. In short, this work might be characterized as a thoroughgoing commitment to the depiction of the accidental. But of course this aspect of his work is frequently missed, precisely because of its success in this escalation of scale. And we are, of course, further blinded to this aspect because of the ubiquity of actual cartoons throughout society, and it is thus tempting, but erroneous, to dismiss Lichtenstein's paintings just as easily. Lichtenstein, however, addresses this point too, that we *are* often ready to dismiss the popular, and such an address is possible only within a context in which cartoons proliferate.

Robert Rauschenberg produced a series of works illustrating Dante's *Inferno*. One way to describe what takes place in that series of images is that two forms of life converge. It is true that in Dante's work itself, one misses a very great deal of the meaning of that text if one is oblivious to the Florentine politics of the day, precisely because Dante settles scores by placing his enemies in positions within the *Inferno* appropriate to their misdeeds. Similarly, if one is blind to the theological aspect, and especially the influence of philosophy in general and Aquinas in particular on the shaping of Dante's mind, one misses the literary portrayal of theological distinctions. And of course, if one overlooks the design, and fails to notice, say, the number of cantos or the use of *terza rima*, one then misses the mastery displayed by Dante through his power to express himself forcefully and evocatively within the limits of self-imposed formal constraints. Likewise, if one looks at one of Rauschenberg's illustrations without knowing the specific cantos to which they refer, one looks without seeing. And if one then further wants to add comprehension to vision, one must add the sociopolitical, theological, and formal aspects mentioned above in such a way that one finds parallels between the visual text of Rauschenberg and the verbal text of Dante. Each of these parallels mark a point of convergence between two forms of life, that is, Dante's Florence and Rauschenberg's New York, with the result that a new location for artistic meaning is developed. And within Rauschenberg's Dante, it is difficult to imagine any specific question of meaning arising that would not find its answer in one of these points of convergence.

Forms of Life and Artistic Practices   75

In the sixteenth century Bronzino painted a remarkable visual commentary, indeed a visual text, on what must have been for him or for his audience the salient moral aspects of love. The *Allegory* ("Venus, Cupid, Folly, and Time") presents in the center an appropriately unclad goddess of love suggestively embracing a similarly disrobed winged Cupid, who in turn delicately caresses temple and breast. To the right is a cherubic boy, representing Pleasure, who looks on in admiring and happy oblivion to what surrounds the central pair. The surrounding figures are a young female figure in a fine green dress, with a quiet, beautiful face but the lower body of a serpent (symbolizing Deceit), a distraught old woman holding her head and tearing her hair (symbolizing Jealousy), Father Time holding back one side of a blue curtain (symbolizing the unveiling powers of time), a goddess opposite Time who is holding back the other side of the curtain (symbolizing Truth), and a pair of masks (symbolizing the distinction between appearance and reality as it applies to this sort of case). First, as with Rauschenberg's illustrations of Dante, if one does not recognize the allegorical references in this work, one simply does not grasp its meaning. Second, the resonance this language has is a function of the experience of the viewer, or, in short, the "common behavior of mankind." Third, that such a theme was both amusing and aesthetically legible to Bronzino's society tells us about that society's sense of humor and, through this, of its concerns. Most important, however, is the process of interpretation itself. One sees first and immediately, and *not* as a function of interpretation, hypotheses-formation, or any visual analogue to the forming of a medical diagnosis, that it is a female figure in the center, a winged-boy next, and so on. It is *after* this foundation is secure that interpretation begins, and this is, indeed, a process of reflection on the "rules" associating the figures with their allegorical significance. The immediate perception is, as Wittgenstein said of the foundational following of rules, "blind"; only later do we begin the process of reading the visual text.

Mondrian produced a well-known group of works in the interest of capturing the purity of Platonic essences. He pursued this goal not in the realm of Ideas but rather on canvas. And on canvas we find not the record of an internal struggle between the mere particulars of things and the Forms of those things themselves but rather designs of great geometric clarity. And these designs are filled with (appropriately) "pure" color. In short, this style of visual purity and clarity, elucidated with a force such that any move threatening or eroding that clarity would be instantly recognized for what it was, an affront to visual essence, was developed within a larger artistic context in which geometric clarity, purity of color, and a narrowly circumscribed range of hard-line abstract gestures were all significant, not only for what they committed to canvas and thus to visual experience, but for what they left out as well. What is present pursues essence and perfection. What is absent, which carries in these works of Mondrian the greatest significance, can only be discerned by placing the work against a background context within which these gestures are striking gestures for purity.

In a manner similar to the merger effected by Rauschenberg of late medieval Florence with twentieth-century Manhattan, Rembrandt produced the deeply engaging painting *Aristotle with the Bust of Homer* in 1653. Aristotle seems to be looking at the sculpted bust, but the bust itself is unseeing; the great blind poet's eyes are lost in the chiaroscuro darkness, and we realize that this darkness is itself sadly and mimetically fitting. Now looking back to the facial expression of Aristotle, we see that his expression is here, as Homer's must be, inwardly directed. It is a state of contemplation that is both inwardly focused and outwardly indicative of the experience of loss. And to see the resignation here portrayed on the author of the *Nicomachean Ethics* is to also see Rembrandt seeing that expression. As Wittgenstein put it, "Look into someone else's face, and see the consciousness in it, and a particular *shade* of consciousness. You see on it, in it...." On Aristotle's face we see the resigned contemplation born of both experience and reflection, and in Aristotle's face we see *Rembrandt's* depiction of that state; to underscore this connection we see that Aristotle is dressed in the garb of Rembrandt's time. Indeed, we see Rembrandt portraying Aristotle's "look" at Homer, which as just described reflects from Homer back to Aristotle, and back to Rembrandt, and—if we do find the work engaging—to ourselves. Here hypotheses that evoke the contractions of facial muscles to explain our perception are as crude as they are obtuse. And if we are "haunted by explanations here," we have indeed neglected "to remind [ourselves] of the most important facts," that when we see emotions, we see emotions and not facial contortions on the basis of which we infer emotions.

In Rembrandt's *Aristotle* we see the depiction of an emotion readily available to us; it is not the case that this expression communicates something hidden from us because of its belonging to a distant or remote historical period. Michael Baxandall has demonstrated, both verbally and visually, how in some cases the significance of expressions *can* in this way be hidden or obscured.[50] He provides an account of Fra Roberto's delineation of five successive mental states that Mary, as depicted in Annunciation paintings, should exemplify: Disquiet, Reflection, Inquiry, Submission, and Merit. These "Laudable Conditions" of the "Angelic Colloquy," as Fra Roberto puts it,[51] once explained and thus acquired as categories within which to shape our visual experience to the original context of the image, have the power to transform our perception of the paintings Baxandall discusses. Simply put, these categories of emotional experience render the depicted expressions immediately recognizable; the initial uncertainty we may feel is thus

---

50. In his *Painting and Experience in Fifteenth-Century Italy* (Oxford: Oxford University Press, 1972).
51. Ibid., p. 51.

not a fact about the need for analogical hypotheses or, indeed, a concept of expression, but rather a fact about what might be described as the emotional distance of a cultural atmosphere permeated by theology. In the case of Botticelli, the errors here become more interesting than the successes, because the naturally emotive gestures depicted fit not a proper miraculous setting, but rather, as Fra Roberto continues, that of "an angel who, in making the Annunciation, seemed to be trying to chase Mary out of her room, with movements showing the sort of attack we might make on some hated enemy; and Mary, as if desperate, seemed to be trying to throw herself out of the window."[52] Human bodily and facial gestures display a power of natural expressivity and significance that overpowers a mere contextual relocation. Gestures, above, were pursued in the interest of bringing out the nonmediated or unconsidered or indeed "animal" characteristic of a form of life, and in that discussion we saw the similarity between understanding negation and understanding a defensive gesture. Botticelli, we might say, has made Mary, within a gesture language, too much concerned with negation.

Wittgenstein says of the ancient rites that they are "a very highly developed gesture-language," and we placed that remark within the larger elucidation of the concept of a form of life. Baxandall also shows in a discussion closely related to the preceding that, to cast the matter one way, fifteenth-century Italian religious painting constitutes a highly developed gesture language. Baxandall quotes relevant instructions for a gesture language from an early sixteenth-century source, in which it is expressly stated that if the matter is solemn, stand upright and point with the forefinger; if cruel, bend the fist and shake the arm; if heavenly, look up and point toward the sky; if gentle, mild, or humble, lay the hands upon the breast; and if speaking of any devotional matter, hold up the hands. With the knowl-

52. Ibid., p. 56.

edge of these expressive conventions, our comprehension of the paintings of Carpaccio, Fra Angelico, Perugino, Pinturicchio, and Botticelli are transformed; what we see is illuminated by what we know, and this knowledge of gesture is, as Baxandall puts it, "a necessary part of looking at Renaissance pictures."[53] The ancient rites possessed a depth that although resistant to propositional encapsulation, both connected thoughts and feelings and exuded a "spirit." With even only a preliminary awareness of the social context of Renaissance painting, we can see that some Renaissance religious painting functions in precisely the same way. We saw earlier Wittgenstein's claim that to "understand a sentence means to understand a language." Here, to understand a gesture means to understand the larger gesture language, the context, in which it functions and operates, in which it has a use.

Raphael's great visual *summa* of Renaissance mental life, *The School of Athens*, has as its center the gesturing figures of Plato and Aristotle. The seeker of transcendental essence, the defender of the realm of ideas available only to the abstract intellect beyond the lower sphere of sensory particulars with their epistemological distractions, looks to his successor with a confident, or indeed knowing, upward-pointing gesture. Aristotle looks with equal confidence back to his predecessor with an outstretched and, indeed, *moderating* gesture, pointing, as it were, to this world. For a defender of the priority of particulars this is indisputably the correct response. But the ideological debate here graphically depicted is understood by knowing something of the influence of these classical authors in Raphael's Florence, and—to state the matter generally—the context within which such gestures are embedded. We saw above, in connection with language, the claim that truth does not merely "hover" above the world and appear as a function of superficial human "agreement in opinions," but rather that with roots

53. Ibid., p. 65.

extending deeply into the practices of a culture, it is "agreement" in form of life. Raphael has found a way to evoke visually, through gesture, what is here indeed a disagreement, and to do this he also evokes, at a deeper level, the agreement in form of life making the metaphysical opposition and its gestural expression possible. Much later, Jacques-Louis David reiterates, in his own way, this visual appropriation of the power of gesture in the *The Death of Socrates*; in this painting we see Socrates reaching for the hemlock unhesitatingly with one hand, and, to give comfort and reassurance to Phaedo, the jailor, Crito and the other witnesses, pointing confidently upward with the other. Here we see the significance if we first know the narrative history of this event from Plato's *Phaedo*, which stands behind the visual history presented here. And we see concerned, compassionate, pained, resigned, and confident expressions beautifully captured by David not mediately, as a consequence of emotive hypothesis-formation, but immediately, as an agreement in a form of life.

That examples could be continued indefinitely is not, I believe, accidental; that examples seem either to embody various detailed aspects of the phrase "form of life" as it is developed in Wittgenstein's philosophy, or that they, in a multitude of distinct ways, enforce the prerequisite of contextual placement for their understanding, itself argues for the contouring of the understanding of art according to our understanding of language as rooted in social practice. To fathom the work in the *vanitas* genre, and to feel almost tangibly the significance of the *memento mori*, is to possess a *sense* of mortality. To comprehend the power of Masaccio's *Expulsion* is to just *see*, as the end of explanation, the expression of irretrievable loss within the context of theology; for its perception actual belief is not necessary, but the ability to imagine that belief most definitely is. If one can understand the possibility of the weariness of the visually sensitive at the culture-wide onslaught of advertising images, one can connect the multiple images of a Campbell's soup can to thought and feeling; moreover, insofar as the critical commentary conveyed by that multiple image suggests that things might be otherwise, that is, that we need not remain the passive receptors of such an onslaught, it thus functions like the "mastery of a technique" that makes hope possible. To recognize the conflicts of divergent conceptions of time, geological, theological, human, animal, immediate, and so on, is part of what is necessary to employ the concept of time, which is in turn necessary to the interpretations, in different ways, of the romantic fascination with ruins, the postmodern employment of the appearance of the weathered, and, specifically, Dali's *Persistence of Memory*. Understanding Giotto's *Betrayal* (The Kiss of Judas) reaches into our knowledge of the unmediated expressive significance of a kiss and, with the understanding of such gestural immediacy as a basis, the terrible moral vacuity of the reduction of that gesture to a mediated, deliberated signal, a convention for betrayal.[54] Here too, although one must know much from human life to comprehend the painting, one need only be aware of the theological content of the painting; it is not necessary to endorse that theology oneself. Again, what is necessary is a capacity to imagine entering into the form of life.

Baxandall, referring to the intrinsic limitations of a purely documentary approach to understanding art, says that such studies "cover some kinds of activity and experience repetitively and neglect others. Much of the most important experience cannot conveniently be encoded into words or numbers." Thus an attempt to encapsulate propositionally the "spirit" systematically misses its mark. He adds, "It is very difficult to get a notion of what it was to be a person of a certain kind at a certain time and place," and against this epistemological difficulty places the remark "It is here that pictorial style is helpful." I would extend this to say that *all* artistic styles help us learn in precisely this way, provided we accept the invitation they extend

---

54. See Rhees, "Wittgenstein on Language and Ritual," pp. 95–96.

to enter them imaginatively, to make an effort to comprehend what it was to be a person of a certain kind at a certain time and place. And this capacity to enter imaginatively an artistic form of life is remarkably like the deeply analogous case of the linguistic capacities to express, to comprehend, to appreciate significance, and to recognize the "spirit" of an utterance.[55] Earlier, we considered, in connection with what was there called the phenomonology of knowing, Wittgenstein's remark "I would like to regard this certainty, not as something akin to hastiness or superficiality, but as a form of life." Capacities for expression, for comprehension, and for the grasping of significance and of "spirit" ought to be regarded in exactly the same way. Taken this way, such capacities themselves weigh against the floating or "hovering" shallowly conventionalist explanations, which themselves both exemplify the belief that language can mean anything the user or receiver wants and, correspondingly, that works of art can mean anything the perceiver sees in them.[56] Indeed, although we can imagine a simple

---

55. It might be pointed out that this is, if in modernized form, not so far from the conceptions of the sympathetic imagination and empathetic understanding as developed in the eighteenth-century moral sense school in which imaginative "entry" takes place in the ethical rather than the aesthetic sphere.

56. To think of the arts as codes or as carriers of "information" attached to various physical media is shallow linguistic conventionalism. Michael Tanner's remark on significance beyond vocabulary and syntax makes it clear that we should avoid such reductive simplicities: "One may feel, reading poetry in a foreign language, that even though one has a mastery of the vocabulary, syntax, and even to some extent the idioms of the language, one is still bound to miss much of the significance of the poetry, because the only way to grasp it is to have spoken the language from the start, living in the community that speaks it" ("Objectivity and Aesthetics," *Proceedings of the Aristotelian Society*, supp. vol. 42 [1968]: 72). In this connection we might recall that it is more than speech alone that is referred to by the term "language-game"; see *Philosophical Investigations*, sec. 7: "I shall also call the whole, consisting of language and the actions with which it is interwoven, the 'language-game'." More extremely, in *On Certainty*, sec. 220, we find: "Our talk gets its meaning from the rest of our proceedings." And further underscoring the fact that speaking is a form of activity situated within a human context, in *Philosophical Investigations*,

code or a floating set of conventional signals—like the superficial agreement on the identifying meaning of Judas's kiss—as a "language," to imagine an *actual* language, with its multiplicity of uses, its ritual-like connections to our thoughts and feelings, its rootedness in social practices, its mediated *and* unmediated employments, and its multitudinous varieties of expressivity, comprehension, significance, and nonexplicit spirit, or in brief its varieties of meaning, is indeed to imagine a form of life.

---

sec. 23: "The word 'language-game' is here meant to emphasize that the *speaking* of a language is a part of an activity or a form of life."

3

～ Circumstances of Significance

There can be very little doubt that Henry James's fiction itself constitutes a richly imagined and painstakingly detailed form of life. Ranging vastly beyond the builders' language, but still providing contexts in which linguistic aims, uses, and functions are vividly represented, James's tales provide expanded microcosms within which to conduct philosophical investigations. In this chapter we examine in detail the specific contents of those fictional circumstances, those repositories of significance, as they are imaginatively depicted in "The Author of Beltraffio."

"THE AUTHOR OF BELTRAFFIO"

Rather than attempt a brief introductory description of a story exemplifying the density and compression of which James was a master, it is better to turn to James himself. In the Prefaces to the New York Edition, he says of "The Author of Beltraffio," having already referred to "the grain of suggestion, the tiny air-blown particle"[1] that constitutes for him the origin of the

---

1. The Prefaces to the New York Edition are reprinted in Henry James, *The Figure in the Carpet and Other Stories*, ed. Frank Kermode (London: Penguin, 1986), p. 49.

work of fiction, that "it had been said to me of an eminent author, these several years dead and on some of the embarrassments of whose life and character a common friend was enlarging: 'Add to them all, moreover, that his wife objects intensely to what he writes. She can't bear it (as you can for that matter rather easily conceive) and that naturally creates a tension—!' *There* had come the air-blown grain which, lodged in a handful of kindly earth, was to produce the story of Mark Ambient."[2]

In the story Mark Ambient is the author of *Beltraffio*, a work much admired by our narrator, a young American who has come to visit the writer at his home, which he shares with his wife, their son, and his unmarried sister. Frank Kermode says of this quartet that within the context, the circumscribed network of possibilities generated by this fictional language-game, that

> the conflict between husband and wife called for an observer, and the observer was characterized as young, "ingenuous" and American, a dedicated admirer of the great Mark Ambient. The battle between husband and wife was to be fought out, naturally enough, over a child. James considered several possible fates for the child, but settled for his death as a victim to his parents' fight for him; or perhaps the mother can deliberately sacrifice him. Once these pieces were in play he introduced another, the sister of Ambient. This done, he wrote the "gruesome" tale at once.[3]

As we shall see, as these pieces are set in play they take on, with characteristic Jamesian detail, lives of their own. A form of life is here being imagined, having been generated out of that initial imaginative seed. And this imagined life has a scheme, a structure or organizing principle, which Kermode

---

2. Ibid., p. 50.
3. In the introduction to *The Figure in the Carpet and Other Stories*, p. 13.

says is "simple and virtually allegorical: the life of art versus the life of evangelical conscience, ending in the sacrifice of life." But having made this general formal assertion, Kermode is immediately driven by a recognition of Jamesian realism, by mimetic complexity, to add, "But the development of the implicit 'relations' greatly complicates the issue." Relations, to be sure, complicate the issue, and in following those relations we discover *circumstances* of meaning, forms of communication and understanding that take place within something that on closer inspection, comes to look rather like a *much* expanded builders' language. Examination of this much expanded builders' language requires sustained attention to detail, but the effort expended is rewarded with what is perhaps a different way of seeing the connections between ethical and aesthetic descriptions and between descriptions of persons and of artifacts and, most important, the complex interrelations between the perception of persons and of works of art. We should move, then, into a consideration of our narrator's ways of describing—and thus ways of seeing—his hosts, their house, and the multifarious relations between these things, people, and descriptions.

Already feeling, on meeting Mark Ambient, "happy and rosy,"[4] while walking together, the American "surveyed him, askance," seeing Ambient "as all delightful." At a glance, in this introductory move in the description of Ambient we already see the relation between the narrator and Ambient and have an expectation of how the description will proceed and what is and is not possible within that description. Following the logic of that continuing description, James gives us these details: "He looked to me at once an English gentlemen and a man of genius, and I thought that a happy combination." This is, of course, not an atomistic perception of physiognomic properties followed by hypotheses about emotional, cultural, and intellectual

---

4. "The Author of Beltraffio," in *The Figure in the Carpet and Other Stories*, p. 60.

properties; it is rather the record of an unmediated impression a person has made on our narrator. It continues, "There was a brush of the Bohemian in his fineness," again a composite perception *not* subsequent to a philosophically motivated scrutiny determined to locate in physical detail evidence to support a hypothesis. A different kind, an authentic and philosophically unobjectionable kind, of scrutiny is taking place here: "He was addicted to velvet jackets, to cigarettes, to loose shirt-collars, to looking a little dishevelled. His features, which were firm but not perfectly regular, are fairly enough represented in his portraits; but no portrait I have seen gives any idea of his expression." James here introduces the Paterian dimension of aestheticism, but he refines it by saying that although the *features* are represented, the *expression* has not been captured.

That our narrator renders this art-critical judgment is significant. This passage does not mean that no portraiture can capture expression and that portrait painters must satisfy themselves with producing merely a likeness of features. Instead, it means that such capturing of expression is *usual*, that Ambient is the exception. That this is an exceptional case of facial expressivity having been established, we as readers now inside this fictional web—this game—expect as the next move the explanation of this facial resistance to depiction that is immediately forthcoming: "There were innumerable things in it, and they chased each other in and out of his face." But this then makes us ask about expressive content, about what is chasing what, and James informs us, "I have seen people who were grave and gay in quick alteration; but Mark Ambient was grave and gay at one and the same moment."

Our narrator continues on the now established topic of the deeper compatibility of seemingly incompatible descriptions: "There were other strange oppositions and contradictions in his slightly faded and fatigued countenance. He affected me somehow as at once fresh and stale, at once anxious and indifferent." Indeed, if handicapped by an unjustifiably narrow conception of what is rationally acceptable in human (or moral) or aesthetic description, a reader confronted with such a case might ask which of the features are real and which are not; that is, which features actually refer to a property of the person or the artifact, and which do not. But in fact, as in this case, such questions are illegitimate; *seeming* incompatibility is not a tension that demands theoretical resolution. The "oppositions and contradictions" *themselves* describe the case before us; and to proceed beyond these descriptions in search of an explanation is not progress. As though engaged in philosophical work, James places these more stark descriptive contrasts next to more familiar and apparently less incompatible specimens in our narrator's next observation: "He had evidently had an active past, which inspired one with curiosity; yet what was that compared to his obvious future?" This is not exactly a contradiction, but rather a break in what might be for others a sense of time's continuity; here Ambient exhibits both a sense of his past and of his future in such a way that our narrator does not know which to speak to first. Further, Ambient "had the friendliest frankest manner possible, and yet I could see it cost him something." Here, inside the game of this densely compressed study of apparent descriptive contradiction, our narrator can see on the one hand that he is fully engaged with his host and that he has been given license to take up and pursue any matter he might like with the senior writer, and on the other hand that he ought not to abuse this license, to employ it recklessly, and that he should exercise some measure of reserve. And this knowledge, this recognition of Ambient's admixture of the "friendliest manner" along with its "cost," itself contributes substantially to the shaping of the relationship between Ambient and the narrator, where this shaping influence—as an article of knowledge born of an aesthetic-like awareness of Ambient— becomes a moral force. Inside the story, the narrator exemplifies a kind of moral sensitivity engendered by an awareness more aesthetic than ethical; beyond the story, James has already established the proximity of ethical and aesthetic sensitivity and commented upon their parallels. But it is to the parallels, the continuities between art and non-art, or—better—the "complicating relations" between art and life that James turns to next, in his narrator's description of the house.

Descriptions In Situ

"There was genius in his house too I thought when we got there; there was imagination in the carpets and curtains, in the pictures and books, in the garden behind it, where certain old brown walls were muffled in creepers that appeared to me to have been copied from a masterpiece of one of the pre-Raphaelites" (p. 61). The narrator sees imagination or imaginativeness in the carpets, curtains, pictures, books, and garden much as we see it in works of art, and he identifies the collective visual force of these as "genius." We know what he means and are prepared for the overstatement because of the "happy and rosy" condition of heightened receptivity we already know him to be in. In short, within this expanding language-game, and because James is giving us enough psychological detail to imagine this form of life, that earlier utterance of self-description here informs, or indeed is "part of the meaning of" (as though there were one such determinate psychological entity), this description of place. And these descriptions of self and of place merge in the conceptual inversion characteristic of aestheticism, the inversion of life and art, that immediately follows his remark that the creepers on Ambient's garden walls seemed to have been copied from a pre-Raphaelite. "That was the way many things struck me at that time, in England—as reproductions of something that existed primarily in art or literature." It is thus imaginative seeing itself—seeing accompanied by associated aspects, or by "thoughts and feeling" as discussed in Chapter 2, that our narrator illustrates; and in his case imagination is fueled by a knowledge of art. This knowledge, as we shall see in what follows, does not merely augment but in fact is his perceptual acuity; here the too-extreme inversion of mimesis is rendered explicit by James in the line "It was not the picture, the poem, the fictive page, that seemed to me a copy; these things were the originals, and the life of happy and distinguished people was fashioned in their image."[5] Here it is becoming increasingly difficult to distinguish between the patterns of description that we find for persons, artifacts, works of art, and places. And a few lines later, we encounter the phrase *genius loci*; the very idea of the spirit of place entails the associated "thought and feelings," the imagination-assisted aspects, in short, the constellation of meanings that constitute the "soul" of the place as an exact parallel to the "soul" of a work of art.

As our narrator passes through the house into the grounds, he describes what he sees in terms that synthesize the human, the artifactual, and the natural. He says that the grounds "covered scarce three or four acres, but ...," which tells us that the place seems much larger than it is: we see the truth of the phenomenological description embedded within the truth of the physical description. This remark, which implicitly disputes the rigid distinction between perception and interpretation (seeing that a thing or place looks larger than it is is an act performed *in* seeing that the thing or place is in fact a specific size), continues, "... but, like the house, were very old and crooked and full of traces of long habitation, with inequalities of level and little flights of steps—mossy and cracked were these—which connected the different parts with each other." Here, as this descriptive game expands, it becomes increasingly difficult to determine whether this perception—this very com-

---

5. This is very probably an instance of James's casting the case in the extreme in order to follow his own advice to "Dramatise it, dramatise it!" See the selection from the Prefaces to the New York Edition, pp. 49–50.

plete and accurate report of perception—is assisted by the imagination or not. To see a mossy cracked step is to see the presence of nature, the presence of a history of use, and through this the presence of the human in the artifactual. To employ the categories of description implied by traditional philosophical categories of perception, to say that in fact our narrator has seen an object first, that it is stone second, that it is shaped by human hands third, that it is cracked, that the crack implies age, that moss further corroborates the hypothesis of age, and so on, is simply a pattern of description that does not fit, does not "map onto," the experience that James reports. Indeed, not only are we not here called on to justify the descriptions by referring to the system of allegedly secure epistemological categories of the directly perceived features, in this passage—a passage from an imagined form of life—we cannot even find where these categories are demarcated. And, as he saw "imaginativeness" in the house, our narrator sees cleverness in the landscape design: "The limits of the place, cleverly dissimulated, were muffled in the great verdurous screens. They formed, as I remember, a thick loose curtain at the further end" (p. 62). Now we see, or are shown, in a passage that resembles a critic's reflection on the characteristics of a work of art, why the place seems larger than it is, and by seeing this we also see the presence of clever dissimulation. And, within this ever-expanding descriptive language-game, the recognition of, or indeed the perception of, these imaginative or human—or aesthetic—characteristics is every bit as rational, every bit as epistemologically secure, as the brute perception that one is looking at land. There is perhaps here a distinction to be made between less and more sophisticated perception, but this distinction does not, within this linguistic context, also carry with it a corresponding distinction in degree of certainty or of descriptive rationality.

This sophistication, this perceptual care, is sustained in our narrator's description of Mrs. Ambient. She "was quite such a wife as I should have expected him to have; slim and fair, with a long neck and pretty eyes and an air of good breeding." That so subtle, so descriptively civilized an observer as our narrator should describe her initially in these physical terms is itself, of course, informative well beyond what it explicitly states. Like every other move we have seen made in this expanded language-game, it conveys far more, through its complicated interconnections to other aims and functions, to other moves made and not made, than what can be read on its surface. Given this game, this context, and given what we have learned of the perceptual and descriptive powers of the narrator, we can conclude that Mrs. Ambient seems to him inaccessible and forbidding in a way Mark Ambient obviously does not. And this impression is verified in the next lines: "She shone with a certain coldness" and in conversation, in her interaction with others, exuded "a certain bland detachment." It is thus the detachment, itself an objectively and readily perceivable feature of her character, that both explains and makes appropriate the initial physical description; it is not a reduction to the physically verifiable that is at issue. There is, however, a kind of verification, a kind of justification (and to this topic we shall return below) in place and at home here; our narrator perceives "a vague air of race" in Mrs. Ambient, and this impression, this perceived aspect, is "justified by my afterwards learning that she was 'connected with the aristocracy'." Thus the "air" is a factual matter, and found as rationally supportable and as certain as the long neck and pretty eyes; for the legitimation of the perception we need not epistemologically *descend* to the physical.

Moves toward aestheticism are made in this description too, but here they have a different function. Allusions to the arts, seeing the arts or some of their aspects in the life being described, were prominent in the characterizations of the "spirit" of Mark Ambient and the spirit of the house. By contrast, with Mrs. Ambient, the phrase "but she was clothed in gentleness as in one of those vaporous redundant scarves that muffle the heroines of Gainsborough and Romney" functions in a different way; it is a description not about "spirit" but about *appearance*. At first glance this description seems identical to the descriptions of Ambient and the house. But inside this game, the phrase must be seen in the light of the words "certain coldness," "detachment," and the more subtle "clothed"—suggesting external covering rather than internal character. The aestheticized description, the analogy to the scarves of Gainsborough, *is* a description of external manner, and within this context stands in stark contrast to the aims and functions of the other aestheticized descriptions, in which the aesthetic and the ethical, the artistic and the personal, are contiguous.

James also gives us a perfect analogy to the word as it operates within this circumscribed context in its various associations to thoughts and feelings in the form of a mimetic work of art—a miniature portrait of Dolcino, the Ambients' son, on a ribbon that Mrs. Ambient wears around her neck. At first, it simply seems a sign of a mother's love of the child and passes in the description of Mrs. Ambient without further comment. But as the story of the battle between the Ambients for the control of the boy unfolds—a battle waged largely by Mrs. Ambient against not so much Mark Ambient as against the evil power she sees motivating his art and manifested in him as artist[6]—this miniature, now seen more properly as an icon, takes on a chilling and symbolic power. It functions, within this game, as an icon of ownership, of possession, of power, and its initial semblance of simplicity and innocence—like the notion that a word might have a meaning independent of game or context—is illusory. Moreover, coming to perceive that such impressions are illusory is also a matter of objective, rational understanding,

---

6. See Kermode's question, "Does the infant's 'more than mortal bloom'... signal to the mother that he should not survive to express, under his father's influence, the evil that, for her, animates all art?" (p. 14).

and the narrator's description of Ambient's sister serves to illustrate this well.

Moving to the extreme cases of Paterian description in this story, our narrator tells us that Miss Ambient's

> appearance was—what shall I call it?—medieval. She was pale and angular, her long thin face was inhabited by sad dark eyes and her black hair intertwined with golden fillets and curious clasps. She wore a faded velvet robe which clung to her when she moved and was "cut", as to the neck and sleeves, like the garments of old Italians. She suggested a symbolic picture, something akin even to Dürer's Melancholia, and was so perfect an image of a type which I, in my ignorance, supposed to be extinct, that while she rose before me I was almost as much startled as if I had seen a ghost (p.73).

It is clear that there can be little doubt that the narrator's characterization of her appearance as "medieval" is justified. He unpacks the term in the context of this description of this particular referent into further descriptive terms and phrases that support his initial judgment, including: "pale", "angular", "long thin face", "inhabited by", "sad dark eyes", "black hair", "curious clasps", "velvet robe", "garments of old Italians", and so on. This aura of a medieval mysterious presence turns out to be deliberate and calculated. Our narrator, having learned of Miss Ambient's concern for outward appearance and having shaped his description to lead us to expect this, says, "I afterwards concluded that Miss Ambient wasn't incapable of deriving pleasure from this weird effect." The ethical significance of this aesthetic depiction is of course already implicit, but a few lines later the narrator renders it explicit: "She was a singular fatuous artificial creature, and I was never more than half to penetrate her motives and mysteries. Of one thing I am sure at least: that they were considerably less insuperable than her appearance announced." It is, naturally, the *tone* of this description that leads us to expect this revelation of the moral through the aesthetic, and this leads us into another dimension of meaning as it functions inside this imagined form of life.

TONE AND GESTURAL EXPRESSION

When the narrator first meets Mrs. Ambient and the boy in the company of Mark Ambient, James shows us that the spirit of an utterance, its tone, informs its meaning as a move in the language-game. As the wife and boy approach, Ambient says, "Ah there she is!" and adds immediately, "and she has got the boy." Our narrator observes at that point that Ambient "noted that last fact in a slightly different tone from any in which he had yet spoken." And this tone being unprecedented, it "lingered in [his] ear." That the utterance should so linger is an indication that there is something distinctive about the particular use to which it is being put, and the tone of the utterance, which contributes to the aim of the move as discussed in Chapter 1, is inseparable in practice from its meaning.

In conversation with Mrs. Ambient, our narrator says of Mark Ambient, "He must have a very happy life then. He has many worshippers." And Mrs. Ambient replies, "Oh yes, I've seen some of them," but then adopts a far-away look "rather as if such a vision were before her at the moment." The fact of her imaginative vision of hoards of admirers is visible to the narrator, as is her estimation of those hoards: "It seemed to indicate, her tone, that the sight was scarcely edifying, and I guessed her quickly enough to be in no great intellectual sympathy with the author of 'Beltraffio'." Of course, all she has said, strictly speaking, is that she has seen some of them. What she has communicated, having used that utterance within this game, vastly exceeds that blunt fact. This move too establishes expectations, and they are fulfilled later in the same conversation when she says, "I'm afraid you think I know much more about my husband's work than I do. I haven't the least idea what he's doing." And then, although this has already revealed a very great deal beyond what propositions in isolation might be thought to convey, "she then added in a slightly different, that is a more explanatory, tone and as if from a glimpse of the enormity of her confession, 'I don't read what he writes'." The magnitude of this utterance, of the confession, *is* enormous because of what that fact signifies about their relationship, their lack of shared vision, their divergent views of the importance of, and the moral value of, literature, and the effects of these conflicts, these varieties of divergence, on the boy. At this point, the narrator begins his project of "converting" her, as he puts it, to a position of admiration and appreciation for Ambient's books, which places him in an ambiguous position, as we shall see, concerning himself as a causal influence on her action; here we see as well a kind of meaning that his questions "Don't you admire his genius?" "Don't you admire 'Beltraffio'?" can take on only within this context.

Much later in the story, the narrator is still hoping to bridge the "gulf dividing them" that was "well-nigh bottomless" (p. 100) and to say something that had the power to "make her change her mind." He remarked that it "seemed an immense pity that so much that was interesting should be lost on her." " 'Nothing's lost upon me,' she said in a tone that didn't make the contradiction less." Here James shows us a case in which it is not only tone that greatly augments what is said, rather it *is* what is said—the words themselves are merely the vehicle for the tone.

The importance of nonverbal communication in "The Author of Beltraffio" is indicated by the emphasis placed on it at the very first meeting of our narrator and Mark Ambient: the narrator reports feeling "transported... when he laid his hand on my shoulder as we came out of the station." In the first struggle between the parents for the boy that our narrator witnesses, there is a vicaress present briefly. The narrator describes her as follows: "She looked at Mrs. Ambient and at

Dolcino, and then looked at me, smiling in a highly amused cheerful manner and almost to a grimace" (p. 66). She is too deliberate, too eager to be agreeable, and too concerned with dispensing good cheer; her ungenuine smile, her near-grimace, communicates far more about herself than she intends. This gestural communication, not lost on our narrator, is followed by the boy telling his father that his mother prefers the boy not to go with his father. This elicits her verbal and gestural reaction: "He's very tired—he has run about all day. He ought to be quiet till he goes to bed. Otherwise he won't sleep." Our narrator remarks, "These declarations fell successively and very distinctly from Mrs. Ambient's lips." To utter these phrases as successive, distinct declarations is to do gestural battle, to which Mark Ambient responds even more powerfully—with a gesture undiluted by verbal accompaniment: "Her husband, still without turning round, bent over the boy and looked at him in silence." He then escalates the conflict to the level of viciousness by asking the boy to choose. The boy answers, "Papa, I don't think I can choose," but then (here again employing tone and gesture to carry his meaning), having made "his voice very low and confidential," adds, "But I've been a great deal with mama today." Ambient, receptive to tone and gesture, says, "My dear fellow, I think you *have* chosen!" and walks off with the boy without further speech. Making moves within the gesture-language that our narrator comprehends, Mrs. Ambient "seated herself again, and her fixed eyes, bent on the ground, expressed for a few moments so much mute agitation that anything I could think of to say would be but a false note." In short, this powerful gestural exchange, and its resultant "mute agitation," precludes speech. The meaning already conveyed is very clear without speech.

When the narrator meets Miss Ambient, an exchange of gestures, not words, establishes the expectations and opens the introductory language-game: "A lady rose from the sofa, however, and inclined her head as I rather surprisedly gazed at her. The ensuing language thus answers the gesture: " 'I dare say you don't know me' she said with a modern laugh. 'I'm Mark Ambient's sister' " (p. 73). And that description "modern" is not left unexplained: "modern—by which I mean that it consisted in the vocal agitation serving between people who meet in drawing-rooms as the solvent of social disparities." Thus the laugh too, within this game, is a gesture with an aim and function specific to this particular context. Later, our narrator reports that this medieval presence "seemed to look at me across the ages" (p. 76). Further investigating the power of gesture within clearly defined contexts, James begins to give the gestures voice. "Miss Ambient's perpetual gaze seemed to put to me: 'Do you perceive how artistic, how very strange and interesting, we are? Frankly now is it possible to be *more* artistic, *more* strange and interesting, than this? You surely won't deny that we're remarkable'." Our narrator then actually objects to the wording of what is only imagined speech, expressive gesture: "I was irritated by her use of the plural pronoun, for she had no right to pair herself with her brother" (p. 77). He has objected to the moral implications of a grammatical detail in speech that never occurs. This has a paradoxical tension only so long as we have a diminished conception of the scope of language and hold cases such as the ones James is giving us at a distance.

A larger conception of language, one that appreciates aim and function within meaning-shaping contexts and recognizes the continuities between verbal and gestural significance, is surely implicitly behind our literary comprehension of further cases of James giving gesture a voice within the mind of the narrator. At one point the boy asks of his father, "Do *you* think me agreeable?" within a context in which agreeableness has been established as a virtue only so long as it does not conceal the truth about whether or not he is recovering from an illness. The boy makes this inquiry of his father, as our narrator tells it, "with the candour of his age and with a look that made his father turn round to me laughing and ask, without saying it, 'Isn't he adorable?' " It would not only be needless and inappropriate to try to isolate verbal from gestural meaning, and then in turn both of these from the meaning-contributing details of the context; it would be impossible. And in the gesture-language, the boy continues expressing himself to the narrator.

"The boy's little fixed white face seemed, as before, to plead with me to stay, and after a while it produced still another effect, a very curious one, which I shall find it difficult to express." Here, James forces us to recognize that gestures, unlike words, can be vague, ambiguous, uncertain, and ineffable. The content of the boy's gesture that the narrator finds difficult to express is nevertheless given approximate form. The "plea I speak of, which issued from the child's eyes ... seemed to make him say: 'The mother who bore me and who presses me here to her bosom—sympathetic little organism that I am—has really the kind of sensibility she has been represented to you as lacking, if you only look for it patiently and respectfully. How is it conceivable she shouldn't have it? How is it possible that *I* should have so much of it—for I'm quite full of it, dear strange gentleman—if it weren't also in some degree in her?" Of course it is vividly apparent that these are not the boy's words, but the narrator's. But they do accuratey depict what we do, in those particular expressive contexts in which a gesture or facial expression moves us to action, to make our action comprehensible as a response to the gestural expression. And this is the point at which the narrator is moved to action in his project of "converting" Mrs. Ambient to an appreciation of Ambient's work: "So it shaped itself before me, the vision of ... putting an end to their ugly difference." And his first step in this direction is rebuffed in a manner that is, within this context and given the moves of this game, as clear and direct as possible: "She gave me a great cold stare, meant apparently as an admonition to me to mind my business." There is, naturally, nothing "apparent" or uncertain about the meaning of this "great cold stare." The word "apparently" as it is used here informs us in yet another context-specific way that our narrator has been blinded by his single-minded enthusiasm for Ambient's fiction.

There are within this imaginary set of "complicating relations" many other illustrations of gestural meaning; for example, at one point, as the ever-curious Miss Ambient speaks to the narrator her "head dropped a little to one side and her eyes fixed themselves on futurity." At another point, providing an exquisite specimen of Jamesian psychological realism, she looks at Mark Ambient in a way that clearly could not be captured better: "she gazed at him from afar—as if he had been a burning ship on the horizon—and simply murmured 'Poor old Mark!' " It is difficult to measure how much meaning would be lost by here reporting only the verbal utterance; one wants to say that those three words alone simply would not be understood.

James presents many further varieties of meaning, which function variously within circumscribed contexts. He often brings out the relations of persons and things obliquely; given our narrator's Paterian sensibility, he often effects this through comparisons to painting: Mrs. Ambient is a Gainsborough or a Romney; Miss Ambient "made up very well as a Rossetti." This shapes our expectations of what their relationship might be like. He gives gestural impressions, such as those made during our narrator's first meeting with the boy, deliberately provisional forms, in order to direct expectations and yet permit revision in accordance with subsequent impressions, as in "it was hard to keep from murmuring all tenderly 'Poor little devil!' though why one should have applied this epithet to a living cherub is more than I can say." Such linguistic moves are, to put it in exclusionary terms, striking for their being so clearly outside the game, as in the "inarticulate comments from my fellow visitor" the vicaress. James extends the topic of tone in such a way that he makes it apply not only to utterances but to places, as in "Oh it has a *tone*," to persons, as in "Surely he has a tone, Mrs. Ambient," and of course to works of art, where the tone is transferred from work to person. He achieves closeness or moral proximity through language without explicitly addressing the topic of proximity, as in "I felt as if within a few moments I had, morally speaking, taken several steps nearer to him." James makes comparison central to the description of persons and works of art, as in "He [Mark Ambient] was the original and she [Miss Ambient] the inevitable imitation," and again, Mrs. Ambient, in contrast to Miss Ambient, is "so the opposite of a Rossetti, she herself a Reynolds or a Lawrence." He offers us a number of exacting descriptions of what is the case by explicitly stating what is not the case, as in his description of Mrs. Ambient as "physically speaking, a wonderful cultivated human plant." James establishes and articulates a mimetic criterion for artistic value, which he elucidates in a language-game of possibility using a "logic" of what is and is not possible for a given character in a given circumstance. On this point Ambient mentions a substandard work of his, *Natalina*, in which "the reconciliation of the two women... could never really have taken place. That sort of thing's ignoble—I blush when I think of it." Within the story itself, the fate of, for example, Miss Ambient is well within the bounds of plausibility: "With her embroideries and her attitudes, her necromantic glances and strange intuitions, [she] retired to a Sisterhood, where, as I am told, she is deeply immured and quite lost to the world." He presents experience as a precondition for understanding and comprehending language[7] in a number of ways, as in "He had said how much he hoped Dolcino would read *all* his works—when he was twenty; he should like him to know what his father had done. Before twenty it would be useless; he wouldn't understand them." It is signifi-

---

7. This fact weighs rather heavily against the view that literary works are hermetically sealed and internally referential.

cant that where James reaches the bounds of description, he presents the very fact of running into the descriptive boundary *itself* as part of the description of the case, as in "Miss Ambient put me indescribably ill at ease," and, in reference to Mrs. Ambient, "I was aware that I differed from her inexpressibly." And finally, as we have seen in connection with the power of gesture, he uses silence itself as a distinct move to great effect within the language-game of "The Author of Beltraffio."

Beyond the investigation into the nature and workings of language as it operates within a specified context, within the imagined form of life that constitutes this story, we are also given a portrayal of a distinct kind of ambiguity that casts further light on the analogy between our understanding of persons and our perception of works of art. Our narrator arrives at this ambiguity concerning his own role in the outcome of this story. The "unspeakable thing" that happens, the grotesque extreme of Mrs. Ambient's desire to possess her son exclusively and to protect him from the perceived harm of his father's artistic influence, is that she dismisses the doctor treating her son's illness and allows the boy to die. In a state of great alarm, Miss Ambient tells our narrator, in the space of a few remarks, that "it's too late to save him" *and* that "you had the idea of making her read Mark's new book!" which is in fact true. Mrs. Ambient read the proofs while sitting with her son behind locked doors, and Miss Ambient explains, "She sacrificed him; she determined to do nothing to make him live. Why else did she lock herself in, why else did she turn away the Doctor? The book gave her a horror; she determined to rescue him—to prevent him from ever being touched." As our narrator fathoms the implication put forward by Miss Ambient, he accurately describes Mrs. Ambient as "cruel and insane." But a certain light has been cast on events so that he, through his efforts to dissuade Mrs. Ambient of her belief in the evil force of literature, is in part responsible: "I dropped upon the nearest bench, overcome with my dismay—quite as much at Miss Ambient's horrible insistence and distinctness as at the monstrous meaning of her words." Indeed, understanding her words forces him to see himself in some way as an agent of tragedy; to comprehend their meaning is to see himself, and his actions, in a very unwelcome and glaring light. And of these words, those enforcers of a way of seeing, he says that "they came amazingly straight, and if they did have a sense I saw myself too woefully figure in it. Had I been then a proximate cause—?"

At the close of the story, James gives us the ultimate inversion of art and life, with Mrs. Ambient, after the boy's death and just before sinking "into a consumption" and soon facing her own, reading *Beltraffio*. And the narrator, trapped in the ambiguity created by Miss Ambient's accusations, sees himself now as unconnected to this unspeakable outcome, and now again as a proximate cause—enmeshed in complicating relations. Appealing to us, he in the end says, "And apropos of consciences, the reader is now in a position to judge of my compunction for my effort to convert my cold hostess." Two divergent and incompatible ways of seeing—like two diverging interpretations of a work of art—have been generated out of diverging collections of descriptions. The presence of this kind of interpretative tension, this oscillation of relational aspects, does not mean that there is not a truth to the matter—even if in particular cases it might be difficult or even impossible to arrive at.

4

Aspects of Interpretation

We have seen that "The Author of Beltraffio" can be read as an investigation into the meaning of Wittgenstein's remark from *Philosophical Investigations*: "Here the term 'language-*game*' is meant to bring into prominence the fact that the *speaking* of language is part of an activity, or of a form of life."[1] James's story "The Lesson of the Master" is also a piece of philosophical fiction, and within its imaginary context ambiguity of aspect applies to—or actually emerges from—both moral and aesthetic description. Indeed, in 'The Lesson of the Master' the distinction between moral and aesthetic description is neither clear, nor regular, nor predictable, for what appears initially to be a strictly factual description of a person turns out *not* to be morally inert, so what appears to be a parallel aesthetic description is not evaluatively or judgmentally inert. In both cases, how the interpretative ambiguity is arrived at is itself a product of the rational assemblage of aspects, of characteristics, of the facts and features of a person or of a work of art—where these aspects are often *relational* in nature—which, taken together,

---

1. Ludwig Wittgenstein, *Philosophical Investigations*, 3d ed., trans. G. E. M. Anscombe (New York: Macmillan, 1953), sec. 23.

constitute a justifiable "picture," a way of seeing, the person or the artifact.

"The Lesson of the Master"

In "The Lesson of the Master" the one to learn the lesson—or lessons—is Paul Overt,[2] a young novelist who has recently produced a novel, *Ginistrella*, to a better sort of critical acclaim. In characteristic Jamesian fashion, we learn a good deal about him very quickly from a collection of descriptions that, as *realistic* descriptions, cut across distinctions of mind and matter, self and other, emotion and reason, inner and outer, and intrinsic property and relational property. James's narrator begins by connecting verbal with aesthetic coherence and between the spirit of utterance with the spirit of place. Overt is shown visiting a country house near London at which he expects to meet the great novelist, the "head of the profession," Henry St. George. Overt has never seen this house before, but when he does see it, he recognizes that it "all went together and spoke in one voice—a rich English voice of the early part of the Eighteenth century" (p. 116). Having thus established Overt's aesthetic sensibility, our narrator tells us that "our friend was slightly nervous; that went with his character as a student of fine prose." Indeed, we learn that Overt "almost shed tears" over the "lower range of production to which [Henry St. George] had fallen after his three first great successes," which, we are told, were followed by thirty-seven novels marked by their "comparative absence of quality." Thus we are not only reminded about the central role of comparison in aesthetic

2. As Kermode observes, "James took care over his characters' names" (Henry James, *The Figure in the Carpet and Other Stories*, ed. Frank Kermode [London: Penguin, 1986], p. 16). "The Lesson of the Master" follows "The Author of Beltraffio" in the same collection, pp. 115–88.

evaluation but also informed about Overt's moral sense. He is genuinely saddened by St. George's aesthetic decline and, further to his credit, is at the beginning of the story "conscious only of the fine original source and of his own immense debt." The narrator adds physical description to help us place Overt more precisely on the human map: he "sauntered vaguely and obliquely across the lawn, taking an independent line." Then having joined a group in the garden, he overhears the remark "It's a nice little place—not much to *do*, you know," and his reaction tells us something about the activity of his mental life: "He felt that he himself was doing so much." Eager to meet St. George, he selects two men who might be "the great misguided novelist," but, exercising thought and scrutiny, and thus telling us more about his perceptual style, disqualifies one as being too young and the other as having "undiscriminating eyes."

Overt is presented here as having "read" facial characteristics in a way that is true to human practices. How he performs this "reading" of facial expressivity has nothing to do with the forming of a hypothesis about an inner state on the evidence of outward physical characteristics. Rather, Overt reflects, or (here again with greater mimetic fidelity) "had a vague sense that the gentleman with the expressionless eyes bore the name that had set his heart beating faster." Here it is the name that triggers an emotional response, which is (1) a function of what Overt *knows* about St. George and (2) most assuredly meaningful—in that the response tells us about both Overt and St. George—although *not* "part of the meaning" of the name. Here, the name "St. George" is operating as a trigger discharging an emotional state ("set his heart beating faster"), where the emotional response in Overt is a function of what he *knows* about St. George. Thus the emotion is activated by cognition, yet this cognition, along with its correlated emotional response, while assuredly meaningful (in that they tell us about both of them), are not "part of the meaning" of the name. A good measure of mental activity occurs here, to include the perception of significant facial features and expressions, but that mental activity is neither the meaning of the words nor the mental content of any intention behind these meanings. Moreover, the understanding of the "sign" would hardly require first brute physical perception, then rule-association, and then interpretation of meaning, as it would indeed require if the familiar extensionalist or physicalistic outer-to-inner perceptual model were accurate.

To correct the misleading appearance of self-congratulation in Overt ("[St. George] would have heard of him, would know something about 'Ginistrella'"), our narrator tells us that Overt had "a dread of being grossly proud" but adds—by way of providing a matter of fact that also functions, in this microcosmic context, as a justification for thinking that St. George would have heard of him—that "even morbid modesty might view the authorship of 'Ginistrella' as constituting a degree of identity," which also illustrates that an external matter of fact—here the fact of authorship—can constitute one criterion of inward identity.

Mrs. St. George strikes Overt as "altogether pretty, with a surprising juvenility and a high smartness of aspect." The descriptions that follow defy ordinary categorization with characteristic Jamesian subtlety. In purely outward terms, she wears an "aggressively Parisian dress." In relation to her husband, she is his "second self." In social "air" she exuded a prosperity that "had deeper foundations than an ink-spotted study-table littered with proof-sheets." In age—and this passage is written almost as if a study in aspect perception—Overt "numbered her years at first as some thirty, and then ended by believing that she might approach her fiftieth. But she somehow in this case juggled away the excess and the difference—you only saw them in a rare glimpse, like the rabbit in the conjurer's sleeve." She displayed a "relaxed attitude in her wicker chair" that "gave a great publicity" to her fine features, and bedecked in "ribbons and trinkets" "looked as if she had put on her best clothes to go to church and then had decided that they were too good for that and had stayed at home." She relates an anecdote about a purchase made in Paris, appears to Overt to "figure great people as larger than life" but then as quickly corrects this erroneous impression by handling a certain Lady Egbert in a "sharply mutinous" way. Having barely glanced at Overt in all this, she reveals to the group that the only thing she ever made Mr. St. George do was to "burn up a bad book. That's all!" Overt is the only writer present, and thus the only person present who, knowing the costs of writing a novel, is sensitive to the utter insensitivity, or the moral significance, embedded in that remark, and he, "irrepressibly" and thus in an unmediated way that is both emotionally and morally expressive, repeats it at her: "That's all!" A moment later, confirming the moral significance of this brief utterance, she mentions that she has also made him "write a few." These statements, however, with their demeaning nonchalance, have begun to reflect on the work of Henry St. George. Yet he is not witness to these remarks because—and here James initiates one of the two primary streams of evidence each plausible unto itself but incompatible with the other in regard to St. George's motivations, running through this story—he has gone to church with Miss Fancourt, daughter of General Fancourt, who is told moreover that "he went to church because your daughter went," and attention is thereby called to "his extraordinary demonstrations to your daughter" (p. 122). Not long thereafter, when St. George and Miss Fancourt have returned, the General makes the first contribution to this evidence-collection: "By Jove, he *is* making up to her—they're going off for another walk."

At this point, Overt sees St. George for the first time, and James as philosopher uses the encounter in the interests of clarity in the philosophy of mind. Overt "felt a certain surprise, for the personage before him seemed to trouble a vision which had been vague only while not confronted with the reality." He sees St. George, realizes on seeing him that his expectations concerning the appearance and countenance of St. George were inaccurate, and yet at the same time realizes that the expectation was *not* an articulated mental image of St. George, because the expectation, although determinate in the sense that it excluded the actual St. George, was vague in that it was not pre-specified. But it is *now* specified, having met with the actual St. George incompatible with it. This is an experience that constitutes the visual analogue to that of "knowing what we want to say" in a given setting and then realizing, after making some utterance incompatible with that intention, that we have not said what we wanted. "What we wanted" is perhaps *now* explicit, now propositionally formulated, as it now stands in contrast to what actually "came out," as we put it. But it still was, for that vagueness, an intention, and that is what, in the form of an expectation, Overt has here. James provides his own analytical commentary on this experience: "As soon as the reality dawned the mental image, retiring with a sigh, became substantial enough to suffer a slight wrong" (p. 123). But it is the continuity of each of the two streams of evidence concerning St. George's real motivations in this part of the story that is of central philosophical significance, and this is returned to with Overt watching Mrs. St. George watching Mr. St. George: "Paul's glance, after a moment, travelled back to this lady, and he saw how her own had followed her husband as he moved off with Miss Fancourt. Overt permitted himself to wonder a little if she were jealous when another woman took him away." This piece of evidence, however, which begins the process of making one interpretation of Henry St. George rationally justifiable, is met immediately with another piece of evidence marking the beginning of the second stream, where his intentions are honorable and where his conversations with Overt are thus sincere: "Then he made out that Mrs. St. George wasn't glaring at the indifferent maiden. Her eyes rested but on her husband, and with unmistakable serenity." This is the first stroke of a different picture, a competing collection of aspects, of the man. Overt, in conversation with Miss Fancourt, finds that she gave him "for half an hour the impression of her beautiful face," and along with this came "a sense of generosity." At dinner, however, he sees that she is once again—and in this context this fact becomes further evidence for the first stream—seated next to Henry St. George. But it is the theme of "reading" a face that is developed at length in the description of this dinner, and through this description one comes to see how remote the inferential model of expressive "reading" discussed earlier is from actual human practice.[3]

He "saw more in St. George's face, which he liked the better for its not having told the whole story in the first three minutes. The story came out as one read, in short installments... and the text was a style considerably involved, a language not easy to translate at sight." It would be difficult to find a clearer case of the analogy between the perception of a face and the perception of a text; moreover, the face-as-text possesses a "literary" style not easily translated. Like language, this face doesn't reveal everything on its surface, and—like the language investigated in "The Author of Beltraffio"—possesses shades; thus "There were shades of meaning in it and a vague perspective of history which receded as you advanced.... Two facts Paul had particularly heeded. The first of these was that he liked the measured mask much better at inscrutable rest than in social agitation; its almost convulsive smile above all displeased him..., whereas the quiet face had a charm that grew in proportion as stillness settled again." And then translating very well even against the stated difficulty of such translation, Overt reflects, "The change to the expression of gaiety excited, he made out, very much the private protest of a person sitting gratefully in the twilight when a lamp is brought in too soon."

3. I am indebted, in the formulation of this problem with its connection to questions of meaning, to Colin Lyas, "The Smile on the Face of the Bloodhound," delivered to the Eastern Division Meetings of the American Society for Aesthetics, University Park, Pennsylvania, March 17, 1990.

Aspects of Interpretation   1 1 1

And now, merging the reading of this facial text with the first-stream evidence, so that in this context-specific way the one *is* the other, Overt adds "that, though generally averse to the flagrant use of ingratiating arts by a man of age 'making up' to a pretty girl, he was not in this case too painfully affected: which seemed to prove either that St. George had a light hand or the air of being younger than he was, or else that Miss Fancourt's own manner somehow made everything right" (p. 127).

Describing Miss Fancourt in a manner that betokens growing emotional engagement—if at this point unknown to the describer himself and thus providing a case in which meaning is entirely severed from intention—our narrator gives us this passage illustrating Overt's special variety of aesthetic scrutiny: "The lines of her face were those of a woman grown, but the child lingered on in her complexion and in the sweetness of her mouth. Above all she was natural—that was indubitable now; more natural than he had supposed at first, perhaps on account of her aesthetic toggery, which was conventionally unconventional, suggesting what he might have called a tortuous spontaneity" (p. 128). This too might be taken as a detailed example of aspect perception, for he sees the child lingering in the grown woman, the sweetness in the expression, the naturalness in the demeanor, the convention in the unconventionality, and—in his distinctive perceptual style—the "torture" in the spontaneity.[4] Further exemplifying this style, he sees, in

---

4. For a discussion of "to see in" and "to see as," see Richard Wollheim, "Seeing-as, Seeing-in, and Pictorial Representation," *Art and its Objects*, 2d. ed. (Cambridge: Cambridge University Press, 1980), and "What the Spectator Sees," in *Painting as an Art* (Princeton: Bollingen, 1987). In brief, seeing the torture in the spontaneity means, in a way perfectly parallel to seeing a figure in the paint, that we do not cease seeing the spontaneity when we see the torture. Wollheim describes this, surely accurately, as a "two-fold" visual experience; my point is that here the same is true of the perception of human characteristics, solidifying the connection between the perception of persons and of works of art. For examples of the dramatic and sudden changes in what

this case *comparing* the aesthetic dimension with the personal and thus comparing sets of aspects, that she "was really more candid than her costume," and a comparison manifests itself once again, here between verbal and literary style, in her telling him that he talks "just like" the people in his book, his having told her much earlier (comparing two related verbal styles) that she talks just like her father. But a return to evidence is brought about by her telling him that St. George has said of his own many recent books that "they're not what they should be" and that "he didn't esteem them" (p. 131). Miss Fancourt's words constitute vividly clear second-stream evidence well beyond what they explicitly state.

Shortly after being given that, however, we see Henry St. George become aware of Overt and Miss Fancourt together in a picture gallery. St. George approaches them from far down the gallery with a "procrastinating air, his hands in his pockets and his eyes trained, right and left, to the pictures." Although he stops *en route* to admire a Gainsborough, we are shown the following: " 'He's going to speak to us!' she fondly breathed.' " The "rapture in her voice" startles Overt, who asks inwardly, giving clearer form to the first stream of evidence, "Does she

---

we see that result when we relate the image before us to another work, see Kirk Varnedoe's discussion of the way we are enabled to see a torso "in" the face of the figures in Picasso's studies for his *Demoiselles* once we situate the face next to the primitive works that inspired this stylistic development, in *A Fine Disregard: What Makes Modern Art Modern* (New York: Abrams, 1990), pp. 200–203. See also his discussion of Degas's *Miss La La*, which, once seen in historical relation to Tiepolo and baroque levitation, reveals itself as being "about ascension," pp. 240–41. In this connection one might recall William James's remark from his *Principles of Psychology* concerning linguistic meaning, that a word possesses "a halo of obscure relations" that "spread about its meaning" (reprinted in John Stuhr, ed., *Classical American Philosophy* [New York: Oxford University Press, 1987], p. 119); in these visually analogous cases one of those obscure relations of the image, through relational re-situation, is rendered vivid. See also Richard Wollheim's discussion of Freud's view of the power of a nonexplicit understanding of what is revealed to us in art, in "Freud and the Understanding of Art," in *On Art and the Mind* (Cambridge: Harvard University Press, 1974), esp. pp. 214–19.

Aspects of Interpretation 113

care for him like *that?*—is she in love with him?" And again seeing one thing in another, Overt says of St. George's apparently casual approach that it is "eagerness dissimulated." A little later, Overt finds himself "for half an hour conjoined with Mrs. St. George," which gives even clearer meaning to the phrase "circumstantial evidence" for the first stream—"her husband had taken the advance with Miss Fancourt, and this pair were quite out of sight" (p. 135).

Through the next section of the story we encounter a good deal of further evidence as we witness Henry St. George in conversation with Overt. He tells Overt that Overt would "give up a good deal" if he were to sacrifice his authorial autonomy and marry. In response to Overt's saying of Miss Fancourt "I like her very much" he excites "on his companion's part a momentary sense of the absurd; he tells Overt that he "*must* be better" and that he "really must keep it up," adding, "I haven't of course." He says of this conversation that "it may serve as a kind of warning"; he invites Overt to witness and learn from "the spectacle of a man meant for better things sunk at my age in such dishonour"; and he adds, "Look at me well, take my lesson to heart—for it *is* a lesson... Don't become... the deplorable illustration of the worship of false gods!" referring to the "idols of the market; money, luxury, and 'the world.'" When St. George says that he has a house in the country an hour from Euston, and that this is one of the reasons his "books are so bad," Overt tries to lighten the tone, by making a joke and laughing. As a heavily weighted piece of evidence for the second stream, St. George "made no direct rejoinder to this"; that is, he refuses to move further in the conversational direction Overt has opened and declines the contextually situated invitation to incorporate levity into this game. And the evidence is heavy, here, because of St. George's refusal to make light of the discrepancy between his authorial achievements and his artistic vision.

But in this conversation, the first stream is not entirely absent.

Of Miss Fancourt, he earlier said enthusiastically, "Doesn't she shed a rosy glow over life?" Of her artistic interests he judges her "an artistic intelligence really of the first order," and then adds, "And lodged in such a form!" And it is only because of the existence of, and the unbroken plausibility of, each of the two streams that some utterances, within this imagined form of life, can be *fully* ambiguous. Of course, it is by now clear that the ambiguity is not "part of the meaning of the utterance," but rather depends on the context; the same words uttered elsewhere could be crystalline in their significance. Here, Overt says, "She's not for a dingy little man of letters; she's for the world, the bright rich world of bribes and rewards. And the world will take hold of her—it will carry her away." St. George replies, "It will try—but it's just a case in which there may be a fight. It would be worth fighting, for a man who had it in him, with youth and talent on his side." The streams meet, creating ambiguity, precisely because St. George might well be encouraging Overt and he might well be reflecting on intentions to recapture his youth and talent. And then of course St. George may well be in possession of an ambiguous or vague intention not unlike Overt's own vague expectation of what St. George would look like, which was rendered explicit only when its inaccuracy became evident; he may be only cautiously and warily formulating such an intention through such ambiguity, where he may indeed be forming—in a way that is given sense by this context—the intention to act against his better intentions. What is surely not ambiguous is that any intentional or mentalistic model of meaning-determination of the sort considered and replaced by language-games in Chapter 1 will not survive application to James's example.

Evidence on both sides continues after this ambiguity-generating merger, when Miss Fancourt says to Overt, "We're going to be friends always. Here he [St. George] comes!", when Overt is literally pushed aside ("giving ground before the pen-

Aspects of Interpretation 115

etration of an elbow"), and when St. George demonstrates a "mystifying little way of alluding to [Mrs. St. George]" (where the sensitivity to the spirit of an utterance constitutes a form of moral sensitivity). Yet St. George is reported as having said independently to Miss Fancourt that Overt's book is "really important" and as talking about Overt's work a great deal and with honest enthusiasm. We see Overt come to a recognition of his love for Miss Fancourt, feeling that he has "tumble[d] into such a well of sympathy" when in her company and, on witnessing her departure one evening with St. George, prolongs a "meditative walk" in Kensington Gardens, sits on the penny chairs and gazes at sailboats, repairs to his club to dine and finds himself unable to order, and goes to the library where he pretends to read an article in an American magazine and, failing to discover its topic, in a dim way senses it to be about Marian Fancourt. These actions, of course, not only serve as evidence for but are in this context descriptions of his emotional state. But it is with a return to St. George that we return again to interpretative ambiguity, although here it arises in the form of the deed instead of the word. On telling Miss Fancourt that he saw St. George visit her last Sunday, she replies "Yes, but it was the last time." This is an utterance dense with meaning, and to grasp that meaning we want, not a consultation into the mental life of St. George, but further evidence; we want to surround it with the other moves in the game. But James only offers moves that possess an equal mixture of power and ambiguity: "The last time?" Overt asks for us. " 'He said he would never come again.' Paul Overt stared. 'Does he mean he wishes to cease to see you?' 'I don't know what he means', the girl bravely smiled." This deed, like the words above, is as it stands impenetrably ambiguous. To find out what it means we would have to follow in literary interpretation precisely the rational process we employ in life: we would have to assemble a better understanding of the aim and function, within this context, of the action, and thus come to see it as one part of a larger fabric of thought and action within which it becomes, as a possessor of significance, intelligible.

St. George's action is, however, not just mysterious; it is ambiguous. And it thus can be construed as further evidence for the second stream, where his moral and aesthetic hopes for Overt are sincere. This stream continues through remarks made to Overt such as "my books...are not a decent subject" and "You're wonderfully on the right road...do you mean to keep it up?" If Overt doesn't keep it up and follows the lead of St. George, "I shall be one of the two or three who know better." In response to high praise from Overt, he responds, "Don't say that; I don't deserve it; it scorches me." "As an artist, I've married for money," here referring not to his wife but to his having "married" a "mercenary muse"; in response to Overt's rejoinder that he must after all have been happy, he replies, "Happy? It's a kind of hell"; and, as the most focused utterance in the second stream, "I'd turn myself inside out to save you" (p. 165) and in response to Overt's query as to what this remark means, he replies—situating the remark within his larger vision of artist integrity and showing the aim of this remark within it—"To make you stick to it—to make you see it through." And we shall see, this is not a careless phrase; the word is "make," not "encourage." Later in this conversation, the function of which is to impart to Overt a more fully elaborated and refined comprehension of authorial integrity so that, within the context of these aesthetic discussions the depiction of the work constitutes a description of the man, St. George says "I've got everything in fact but the great thing... the sense of having done the best." And he then consolidates his lesson for Overt with what seems to be a paradox, a perfect inconsistency, and what is, within this much-expanded game, a perfectly succinct statement of his aesthetic station: "I've had everything. In other words I've missed everything" (p. 169). But in what follows, the streams again meet for more than just a few remarks, and James here gives us a conversation that can be read as pure sincerity or pure manipulation.

Having told Overt that he cannot have what is best without sacrifices, and having lapsed into self-mockery in a way that here reinforces that claim (for example "Study me well. You may really have horses"), he then places Miss Fancourt in direct and irreconcilable opposition to authentic artistic achievement. "Are you in love with her?" "Yes," replies Overt. Then, bluntly, St. George squares the opposition: "Well then give it up." In the discussion that follows it is clear that what has become not only the analogy between but in fact the mutual identity of aesthetic and moral description is employed to force Overt to act in a way consistent with the self-definition he holds. Recall that he looks forward to his next—and even much better— novel, and he is moved almost to tears by the case of St. George. He has learned his lesson well: he is now, given the galvanizing effect of his conversations with the misguided master, unable to amend even slightly his strict policy of authorial solitude without having that gesture constitute a wholesale forfeiture of his ethical and aesthetic identity. Making manifest the moral necessity intrinsic to this context, he says, looking into St. George's "strange deep face," "No, I *am* an artist—I can't help it!" And then making a move that is either the epitome of sincerity or the most vicious manipulation, St. George says, "Let me see before I die the thing I most want, the thing I yearn for: a life in which the passion—ours—is really intense. If you can be rare don't fail of it!" And with an action functioning as an unassailable conclusion to an argument, verifying the self-definition given content by their mutually developed conception of ethical and aesthetic integrity, Overt leaves England for a long absence "full of brave intentions" (p. 175).

Working on the successor to *Ginestrella*, Overt returns to Lake Geneva, "a region and a view for which he had an affection that sprang from old associations and was capable of mysterious revivals and refreshments," a place that is for him meaningful and that possesses a sense of depth because of its connections to thoughts and feelings, a place with indeed a "spirit" that influences him as do the works of art and the persons with which we have already seen him engage. And it is here that he learns of the sudden death of Mrs. St. George, and of Henry St. George's reaction to this event. Even though Overt is in possession of all the raw material we have out of which to assemble competing and incompatible views of St. George, even though he has been in the presence of both streams, he has only seen one—the second. The first stream is not made visible until now, until the interpretative shift—like the dawning of an aspect—is effected by St. George's epitaph for his wife: "She carried on our life with the greatest art, the rarest devotion, and I was free, as few men can have been, to drive my pen..." (p. 177). Of course Overt expects bereavement, but this particular way of expressing it acquires a shading, for Overt and within the confines of the history of their exchanges, of "contradiction" or "retraction." And for the first time giving definite form for himself to the interpretative ambiguity and thus switching on the oscillation of sincerity and manipulation, if St. George means what he says now, then "what in the name of consistency had the dear man meant by turning *him* upside down that night—by dosing him to that degree, at the most sensitive hour of his life, with the doctrine of renunciation?" Because—and he now can begin to sense at a distance the burning urgency this matter of moral logic might later assume—"if St. George is correct *now* then renunciation was a mistake." Although Overt contemplates returning immediately to London to take action against this doctrine of renunciation and thus implicitly to construe St. George according to the second stream, he does not. As he is placing his manuscript-in-progress into his portmanteau, he catches a glimpse of it and finds, to his pleasure, "high promise," where of course what it promises is the fulfillment of the aesthetic vision inculcated by the St. George of the first stream. James gives us here a vivid illustration of the moral force of an aesthetic perception: Overt stays to finish the novel.

Two years later Overt returns to London, passes by a place here again rich in meaning for its connections to thought and feeling, and encounters by chance one of its occupants, General Fancourt. From him he learns that St. George is to be married soon, and moments later in the conversation Overt, "to whom something had occurred which made his speech for the moment a little thick," also has this feared thought, which throughout that evening "passed over him like a hot wave," the phenomenology of which renders doubtful any attempts to distinguish in a general or unitary way the cognitive from the emotive. The question framing the interpretative ambiguity that he felt from a distance almost two years before is thus fully ignited: "Was it a plan—was it a plan? . . . "Have I been duped, sold, swindled?" And here again written almost as a study in aspect perception, we are told that "he felt as if some of the elements of a hard sum had been given him and the others were wanting: he couldn't do his sum till he had got all his figures" (p. 182). James has here captured the logic, the rational procedure, that operates in practice, in situ, and that allows us to assemble an interpretation, a view, of a person—and as I have suggested throughout of a work of art as well—and to find it highly likely, probable, acceptable, provisional, doubtful, suspect, partially any of these, or any other of the very large number of specific interpretative positions in the epistemological space between the definitely certain and the certainly erroneous.

In one of these intermediate positions Overt, as a way of testing his first-stream hypothesis, confronts St. George, saying in reference to what was for him their decisive conversation, "No wonder you said what you did." But shifting back toward the point of plausibility in the second stream, St. George says, "In the light of the present occasion? Ah but there was no light then. How could I have foreseen this hour?" and hedging toward probability, adds in response to whether he thought this outcome had struck him as a likelihood, "Upon my honour, no." Responding as we do, in visual terms where the issue concerns the "light" in which something is "seen"—thus further underscoring the applicability of aspect perception to persons, to character—Overt says "I see—I see." Nevertheless, the younger author reverts to the first stream, telling St. George that he should be ashamed of his reasons for his actions in connection with Miss Fancourt. St. George, with a facial expression of particularly pointed meaning in this context, "beautifully smiled" and said "You must let me be the judge of them, my good friend" (p. 186). And further in self-defense, he says that he couldn't pierce futurity—thus employing an epistemological limit as a corresponding limit in moral interpretation—and finally, directly, and confirming the impression the beautiful smile gives, "I wanted to save you, rare and precious as you are." Overt, putting matters face-to-face, asks, "Are you marrying Miss Fancourt to save me?" And, with Jamesian complexity, St. George replies, "Not absolutely, but it adds to the pleasure," and says, employing the word "making" both in the sense of "forcing" Overt to take the higher aesthetic course and in the sense of "constructing" the young artist, "I shall be the making of you." But St. George has after all *himself* regained the artistic autonomy he believes to be prerequisite for "the best thing," and has as quickly sacrificed it—if that is what it is—in favor of Miss Fancourt, and Overt is now painfully aware of this.

With words and deeds diametrically opposed, where each appears as strong evidence for incompatible interpretations of the man, St. George says, "Consider at any rate the warning I am at present." This is the same utterance as that contained in his lesson years earlier, but it here, with changed circumstances, cannot have the same meaning. Here it argues for manipulation, against sincerity, and Overt thinks, "This was too much—he *was* the mocking fiend." Employing gesture in place of the language he will no longer use, meaning that he will no longer establish possibilities, openings, for St. George to speak in self-defense, Overt gives "a mere nod for good night" (p. 187) and takes his leave, seeing that he might "come back to [St. George] and his easy grace...[at] some time in the far future," but knowing that he "couldn't fraternize with him now." Overt reflects, much later that night, that if St. George at the end of a year puts forth something "finer than his finest," he will indeed have been "diabolically 'sold'." This of course suggests that if St. George does not in fact return to a higher production, that the other stream will be confirmed; in any case, at the end of the story Overt, a season later, "doesn't even yet feel safe." And of course it is possible, and in a way that would lend force to this being described as James's first *fully* ambiguous story,[5] that St. George himself doesn't know which stream of interpretation is the truth.

Early in the story, when Overt is engaged in conversation with Miss Fancourt, he says of St. George's art that "for one who looks at it from the artistic point of view it contains a bottomless ambiguity" (p. 152). James has shown that this description applies with equal force to St. George's life and has given us a better and deeper understanding of the word "ambiguity" itself, an understanding not of any unitary meaning, but of the significance it has acquired not only within the immediate context within which it has a function but, beyond this, from the history of the moves made in the extended game or family of games of which the present use is a member.

Of the ambiguous drawing that can be seen as a sketch of a duck, or of a rabbit, Wittgenstein said, "Had I replied 'It's a rabbit', the ambiguity would have escaped me." If one did not know the detailed history of the conversations Overt has had with St. George, and of his influence on Overt's actions, and of his own history in connection with Miss Fancourt, one would

---

5. See Kermode's discussion in his introduction to James, *The Figure in the Carpet and Other Stories*, p. 15.

similarly miss the ambiguity of St. George. Indeed, we might imagine the description—the very simple and shallow description—of St. George that we might have given in the absence of such detailed knowledge, and then contrast that with what we now "see." Given those extensive Jamesian descriptions, and given the histories of their intersections we now know, our vision of St. George is profoundly altered, and, as Wittgenstein puts it a bit later in the same discussion, "I *describe* the alteration like a perception; quite as if the object had altered before my eyes."[6] St. George, as we assemble the picture of him, the oscillating ambigous picture that James has provided, seems to alter before our eyes—just as he alters before Overt's eyes.

Wittgenstein mentions as well the close relation between seeing a likeness and noticing an aspect: "I contemplate a face, and then suddenly notice its likeness to another. I *see* that it has not changed; and yet I see it differently" (*Philosophical Investigations*, p. 193). In contemplating the "face," the depiction, of St. George, one reader may see a likeness to other cases of insincerity or manipulation early on in that narrative depiction, whereas another may not. The literary depiction, which exemplifies the patterns of the moral understanding of a person and the aesthetic understanding of a work of art, has not changed, and yet it is indisputably seen differently. At this point a sort of radical subjectivism threatens to break into the discussion of the logic of interpretation, it is this temptation to interpretative relativism that Wittgenstein exposes when he warns his interlocutor "And above all do *not* say... 'After all my visual impression isn't the *drawing*; it is *this*—which I can't show to anyone'" (p. 196.). Concerning "The Lesson of the Master," we can imagine Wittgenstein warning us *not* to say that it is not the realistic narrative depiction of St. George that

6. This and the surrounding passages are from the extended discussion in *Philosophical Investigations*, pt. II, sec. xi.

constitutes my impression, it is *this*, referring to an inner, subjective, object of interpretation. Wittgenstein adds, "Of course it [the visual impression, or, in our case, the narrative depiction] is not the drawing, "but neither is it anything of the same category, which I carry within myself" (p. 196). Much of the trouble, then, and the temptation to explain dualistically,[7] arises from the seating of a familiar referential model of meaning, that is a model of atomistic or outwardly "hard" objects that later become the outward correspondences of inwardly "soft" interpretative entities, into the present issue of literary interpretation. But if the "impression" is "not anything of the same category" that we carry within ourselves, what is it? Wittgenstein is making clear that "the concept of the 'inner picture' is misleading," because "this concept uses the *'outer* picture' as a model." *That*, indeed, is the problem, and the belief that objectivity, in aesthetic, ethical, or for that matter scientific dimensions, must strictly concern itself with the depersonalized identification of hard, stable, outward objects is a positivistic mythology that nothing less powerful than a vivid awareness of the complexities of actual perception and description, complexities of the sort that, within their delimited contextual uses, are unproblematically *functional*, will help us overcome.

In readings of "The Author of Beltraffio" and of "The Lesson of the Master," readings that must of necessity be close and detailed if the conception of language developed in Chapters 1 and 2 is accurate, we saw descriptions of characters crossing all metaphysical borders in unpredictable and, indeed, context-specific ways. They included, in any and all combinations, mental, physical, emotional, cognitive, historical, immediate,

---

7. Well beyond the detailed and specific cases of James's short stories that I am considering here, literature very often serves to diminish this reductive temptation. See, for example, Lionel Trilling's acknowledgment of this fact: "Literature is the human activity that takes the fullest and most precise account of variousness, possibility, complexity, and difficulty" (*The Liberal Imagination* [1951; Harmondsworth: Penguin, 1970], p. 14).

spoken, unsaid, fully, partially and minimally articulated expectations, and equally divergent and multifarious satisfactions—or the reverse—of these expectations. We saw descriptions of demeanor, verbal style, walking styles, seating placements, gestures, things left unsaid, comprehension, incomprehension, doubt and suspicion, the repression of doubt and suspicion, gain, loss, sacrifice, postponement, and a multitude of other human practices that refuse to cooperate with the simplifying and simultaneously obscuring interpretative epistemology of the inner and the outer. With the vivid awareness of these complexities[8] and emergent patterns of complexities that James consistently captures, we are better able to see our way clear of the "misleading model of the outer picture" and its more obvious counterpart, the model of the inner, private, and subjective interpretation. And that obvious counterpart is not merely one peripheral by-product of interpretative relativism; it is its essence, its theoretical core.

Wittgenstein remarks that the experience of seeing-as is both like and again not like seeing (*PI*, p. 197). Because of this, a perceptual experience of this variety "seems half visual experience, half thought." This latter remark is very easily misunderstood. The word is, after all, *seems*, yet this can be erroneously taken as an endorsement of the simple additive model that he is in fact escaping through an appreciation of the complexities of practice. If indeed all such cases *were* simply cases in which thought, or inward, post-perceptual interpretation, joined its outward, brute-perceptual base, then we would be entitled to ask general questions, and expect general answers, about the relations that hold between the outward object of attention—be that object or person or work of art—and the inward depiction or impression of it of the sort much discussed in dualistic theories meaning and of

---

8. The implicit suggestion here is that literature more frequently than philosophy engenders vivid awareness of complexity; I return to this topic explicitly in connection with epistemology in Chapter 5.

perception. And with this traditional gap between matter and mind, between the text and its interpretation, the candidates for general answers seem apparent: either there is a direct verifiable correspondence, yielding aesthetic realism, or there is not (in such a way that two or more incompatible interpretations can be simultaneously verifiable), yielding aesthetic relativism. But again, such cases *seem* half visual experience, half thought. When we look at the complexity of the descriptions of those experiences in situ, as James does, we see that the rational procedures, invariably altered to suit the circumscribed demands of the case, that we follow in assembling a "picture" of a person or of a work of art, in assembling an understanding of the person's motivations or the work of art's contextual function, or in assembling an appreciation of the significance or depth of an utterance are not accurately or adequately mapped by a simple additive dichotomy.

When Overt confronts St. George, St. George "beautifully smile[s]." When he speaks to St. George earlier, he looks into his "strange, deep face." These are philosophically significant Jamesian descriptions of facial interpretations. Suppose, Wittgenstein asks, someone were to say, "Something about his face struck you just now"... "Is being struck looking plus thinking?" (*PI*, p. 211). For reasons we can now see, he answers: "No. Many of our concepts *cross* here." In the same discussion Wittgenstein also makes the now-famous remark "What I perceive in the dawning of an aspect is not a property of the object, but an internal relation between it and other objects" (*PI*, p. 212). It is true that this too is easily misunderstood because of its perilously close proximity to the dualistic scheme placing physical objects at the verifiable base of an epistemological hierarchy. But it is only *close*; the point is that in moving from a description of an object's properties to a description of its relational properties, its role, station, or function within a context we are *not* thereby moving from one realm of the objective, to another epistemogically or critically second-class realm of the

126   *Meaning & Interpretation*

subjective. Whether or not St. George is related to Mrs. St. George, or to Miss Fancourt, are factual matters that can be settled decisively, although not by just *looking* at the man on first appearance outside any context or, as it applies to this case, outside an imagined form of life. And once settled through a process of rational inquiry, they are thus immune to relativistic incompatibilities. This is true of St. George, it is true of the descriptions of St. George as being "morally ambiguous," and it is true, through a similar process of comparison and indeed through the perception of relational properties of the sort illustrated so finely in "The Author of Beltraffio," of the phrase "fully ambiguous" as it applies to "The Lesson of the Master." This is, simply put, the isomorphism that exists between ethical and aesthetic reasoning, as it advances through multifarious descriptions,[9] which James has if not said then most certainly shown.

This multitude of descriptive complexities, because they are after all *descriptions*, constitutes one part of the larger picture, the larger landscape, of language as it was discussed in Chapters 1 and 2. But in this, as in any landscape, one can know one's way about or not. James, I suggest, most assuredly does. But how do we tell if someone is seeing the person, the history of action, the evidence, or the work of art, the history within which it has a place, the plausibility of its critical directives, in the same way we are? As we have seen, the description itself carries its way of seeing; thus to follow a description, and to comprehend its significance, *is* to see it in a certain way. This does however, stated generally, again make the matter appear sim-

---

9. Wittgenstein in fact offers throughout these pages of *Philosophical Investigations*, as part of an analysis of perception, a demonstration of the power of description and its role as a criterion for interpretative objectivity. If we are invited to see a sphere in a painting floating instead of lying, how do we determine whether it is "really a different impression" (p. 202)? We do not analyze our own inner experience (p. 204); rather we say that we "describe what [we are] seeing differently" (p. 202).

pler than it is. Wittgenstein remarks that if one cannot see a drawing in descriptive geometry in a way according to its function in such cases one doesn't " 'know [ones] way about' too well" (*PI*, p. 203). And he adds, "This familiarity is certainly one of our criteria." In interpretation and criticism, even the most extreme relativist would have to allow a distinction between someone who, as we say, knows what he or she is talking about and one who does not. But this distinction is not made on the basis of one's ability to either state the verifiable properties of an object or to articulate the details of an inner impression; it is a distinction made, rather, on the basis of "knowing one's way about." "What tells us that someone is seeing the drawing three-dimensionally is a certain kind of 'knowing one's way about'. Certain gestures, for instance, which indicate three-dimensional relations; fine shades of behavior" (*PI*, p. 203). Fine shades of behavior are precisely what James has put on display, and every case of such shading—like the nuances of the contextual shading of the meaning of a word—serves to indicate a difference in perception, in understanding, in comprehension, in significance. And those shades, where they indicate fine differences and distinctions of perception, thus indicate how what is being perceived or described is going to be taken, and in the case of St. George, how it is going to function as evidence. Thus "one *kind* of aspect might be called 'aspects of organization'. When the aspect changes parts of the picture go together which before did not" (*PI*, p. 208). Although this was written as part of Wittgenstein's analysis of seeing-as, the same phrase might have served as a commentary on Overt's later reflections on St. George. That it could so serve further reinforces the parallel between the equally rational processes of forming a "picture," collecting a cumulative set of reflections, observations, properties, relations—in short, all that our descriptions include—of a person and of a work of art.

There is still another sense in which the different parts of our picture of St. George may go together. "Indecision," "uncertainty," "ambivalence," and "unclarity of motivation," only hinted at within each of the separate streams, may serve as aspect-organizing descriptions that bring elements of the first and the second stream together (thus constituting a third stream, in fact), giving St. George's meaningful smile and final remarks again new significance. He may be initially utterly unclear about his own intentions; he may, unbeknownst to anyone, including himself, be engaged in both projects. He may indeed be joining us, adopting our position—but with regard to himself—as active participants in a larger community of understanding in which we contextualize a particular piece of physical behavior, or a particular set of words, into a meaning-determining pattern, history, picture, or indeed stream. He may wonder at himself, trying different contextualizations at different times, feeling the pull of both ways of rendering his actions intelligible, and recognizing—with a self-reflective smile and a correlated desire to articulate ambiguity itself clearly—that his own actions require for their explanation a new picture, a new organization of aspects, a third stream. To put it slightly differently, we may understand St. George correctly if we recognize the aspectival ambiguity and *preserve* it, within a larger organizing picture of indecision and reflexive unclarity, rather than striving to assess the evidential force of each of the streams and choosing the stronger, maintaining all the while the presumption that we must choose in order to understand. We cannot know, in advance of our active processes of the interpretations, contextualizations, and understandings of words and of deeds, which parts of the picture, or even which categories or groups of parts, "go together." We must, in a case-by-case and context-specific way, both look and see.

Deeper into the discussion just above Wittgenstein observes that he can imagine an arbitrary cipher (*PI*, p. 210.), an example of which he draws, and that he can imagine it to be a correctly written letter of one foreign alphabet, or an incorrectly written letter of another. It could be imagined to deviate from a (nonexistent) correct counterpart in a variety of ways. And he adds the reflection, especially significant within the context of this discussion, "And I can see it in various aspects according to the fiction I surround it with. And here there is a close kinship with 'experiencing the meaning of a word'." That kinship, of course, we have already seen with the requisite context-specificity throughout this chapter. And although it would be nice to summarize the kinship, to conclude the matter by giving it a succinct generalized encapsulation, it would be an error. For this kinship manifests itself diversely over the range of our actual ethical and aesthetic discourse, our "everyday" moral and critical language-games, which themselves represent the continuum of epistemological stations from the definitively certain to the utterly unacceptable. Earlier in the discussion of perception Wittgenstein said, "What we have rather to do is to accept the everyday language-game, and to note *false* accounts of the matter *as* false" (*PI*, p. 200). This is not, of course, an invitation to accept an article of philosophical methodology on faith. It is an invitation, extended for good reason, to remain vividly aware of what we know.

AGAINST REDUCTIONISM

Within the context of his discussion of perception, having distinguished between "the 'continuous seeing' of an aspect and the 'dawning' of an aspect" (*PI*, p. 194), Wittgenstein observes that it would make no sense to say, "at the sight of a knife and fork 'Now I am seeing this as a knife and a fork'." These remarks move us from a discussion of unstable perception, that is, cases within which we encounter oscillating aspects, to a discussion of stable perception, that is, cases in which no perceptual *shift* is possible. He adds to the above remark, "This expression would not be understood. —Any more than: 'Now it's a fork' or 'It can be a fork too'." The stability of the fork thus renders this last move in the game incoherent.¹⁰ Do we face a parallel conceptual-linguistic limit when discussing perception in the arts? It takes little imagination to see that the answer is affirmative: we cannot stand before La Gioconda, for example, and say "Now it's a painting" or "It can be a portrait too." Nor can we say, while reading a work of James's, "Now it's a work of literature" or "It can be a work of fiction too." By casting light on the nature of our perception of the arts in this particular way, by asking a very general question about how it is we most fundamentally perceive art objects in order to engage with them as we do, we can profitably make still another analogical move, by now entirely familiar, to the case of perceiving persons. Before doing this, however, it is instructive to pause to reflect on how remarkably easy it would be at this juncture to fall into error of one variety or another.

We might, for example, say that we want an answer to the question asking how it is we take an object as a work of art. But this way of putting the matter, of framing the question, applies only to certain peripheral cases, such as porcelain fixtures, where a "Duchampian question" arises. We might ask what it is we add over and above the physical object, or what nonmaterial, cultural, or emergent properties we perceive

10. Scruton's discussion of the differing designs of two forks and their differing aspects and cultural significance illustrates this well; the fact that the subject under discussion is a fork does not change, although the descriptions of course do. The stability of the fork thus precludes any such locution as "Now seeing the object as a fork, it..." (*The Aesthetics of Architecture* [Princeton: Princeton University Press, 1979], pp. 241–42). Also, this work contains a demonstration of how understanding a work of architecture results from describing its features without acknowledging a distinction between hard fact and interpretative aspect. See Scruton's discussion of Borromini's *Oratorio di San Filippo Neri*, pp. 120–24, in which Scruton uncovers the fact, highly significant for our understanding of aesthetic reasoning, that once one has seen a work in a given "light," or as a collection of particular features or aspects, one cannot then whimsically adopt one position or another in regard to the aesthetic evaluation of that work. He also shows one of the ways in which moral and aesthetic reasoning, that is to say ethics and aesthetics, are one.

"above" the work, thus reiterating within the formulation of the question the dualistic metaphysics separating mind from matter that is thoroughly familiar to aesthetic theory. We might further ask how it is that we answer a conceptually prerequisite doubt whether that object is or is not a work of art as though such a doubt were in fact operative in every case. And we might ask how it is that we see—continuously see—an object as a work of art, thus insisting on conceptual-linguistic room to make the move that we have just seen, in Wittgenstein's observation that we can't see a fork *as* a fork, is in fact contextually proscribed. Again, such a move is possible within a context where a piece of driftwood figures centrally, but not where the *Mona Lisa* so figures. With that cautionary note concerning the remarkable ease of error one faces in this conceptual vicinity, of the danger of misformulation and the subsequent aesthetic theory shaped by the rigid distinction between matter and mind, we can turn to the question—dangerously put—of how it is we perceive, not gestures, facial expressions, utterances, contextually sited expressive shadings and nuances, characters, moral intentions, or styles of interactions but rather *persons themselves.*

In *Philosophical Investigations* (pt. II, sec. iv), Wittgenstein states the case "I believe that he is suffering," and then asks, "Do I also *believe* that he isn't an automaton?" Of course, *belief* is the wrong tool for the job, and he adds, "It would go against the grain to use the word in both connections." The grain, we might here well be inclined to think, is the certainty that makes "belief" too weak. But this, in fact, is another opening into an avenue of error. Hence Wittgenstein's parenthetical remark "Or is it like this: I believe that he is suffering, but am certain that he is not an automaton? Nonsense!" This avenue would lead again to the conclusion that we have already found unacceptable through a detailed consideration of Jamesian descriptions of perception, that we are justified in the hypothesis that we have before us a person because we see before us a body before us behaving in a way that we have come to associate with the idea of a human being. But the more important issue here is the doubt that allegedly motivates our movement along this avenue of thought to this conclusion. The doubt is, as we saw earlier, out of place, and thus we do not *believe* that the man before us is not an automaton, nor are we certain he is not. Nonsense, as we saw in Chapter 1, is often an illegitimate move made within a circumscribed game which, nevertheless, has the appearance of legitimacy, of *working*, of having an aim and function within the given context. Wittgenstein places this move into an imagined context to expose its pretensions by saying, "Suppose I say of a friend: 'He isn't an automaton'.— What information is conveyed by this, and to whom would it be information? To a *human being* who meets him in ordinary circumstances? What information *could* it give him?" Crucial here, and emphasized for this reason, is the phrase "human being"; this is, despite what one would be led to believe through an application of the too-familiar rigid distinction between mind and body to aesthetic perception, *not* a hypothetical entity composed of a collection of mixed mental and physical attributes. The nature of our interaction, of our engagements, with human beings is seriously miscast by this model,[11] and it is the reality over and against this miscasting that Wittgenstein is pursuing in these remarks. He says, " 'I believe that he is not an automaton', just like that, so far makes no sense." And as we have considered the close analogy between the perception of a person and the perception of a work of art at a number of their points of intersection, saying, "I believe that this is not a mere artifact," or, better, this is *not* "not a work of literature," just like that, makes no more sense. But if not a matter of belief, or a matter of certainty, what then can we say without opening

---

11. See Anthony Palmer's illuminating discussion of this model, which he rightly terms "grotesque," in connection with focused issues of linguistic meaning, and particulary of its pernicious and usually unrecognized influence on the shaping of the problem of the unity of the proposition, in *Concept and Object* (London: Routledge, 1988).

at least a passageway into conceptual error about the nature of this interaction, this engagement, with persons that will cast light on the nature of our interaction and engagement with works of art? Wittgenstein next remarks, "My attitude towards him is an attitude towards a soul," to which he adds the avenue-closing remark "I am not of the *opinion* that he has a soul." Similarly, we are not of the *opinion* that the *Mona Lisa* is a portrait or that "The Figure in the Carpet" is a work of fiction. But to use the word "attitude"[12] in any aesthetic context now opens the floodgates of suspicion. Is there a way of employing it helpfully without lapsing into error here too?

An attitude toward the soul, *eine Einstellung zur Seele*, will, properly understood, extend more deeply into our practices as they are embedded in our form of life, and in an essay of this title Peter Winch shows how the meaning of the word "attitude," as it is employed in these remarks in part II, sec. iv of *Philosophical Investigations*, excludes both matters of belief and of certainty.[13] And he shows, against a misinterpretation invited by the word "attitude," how such an attitude is not a "subjective" matter, not the sort of thing we can take up or put down, adopt or deny, at will. Winch, relating this use of the word to a similar use in *Philosophical Investigations* (sec. 310), in which Wittgenstein discusses the attitude we hold toward someone who tells us he is in pain, advises that if we want to understand such expressive phenomena, "We should not allow ourselves to be hypnotised by... verbal expression ... but should look at the whole range of behaviour, demeanour, facial expression, etc. in which such verbal expressions are embedded, and with which they are continuous, which give the words their particular sense and

---

12. See Jerome Stolnitz, "The Aesthetic Attitude," in *Introductory Readings in Aesthetics*, ed. John Hospers (New York: Macmillan, 1969), and George Dickie, "The Myth of the Aesthetic Attitude," also in Hospers, ed., *Introductory Readings in Aesthetics*.

13. "*Eine Einstellung zur Seele*," in *Trying to Make Sense* (Oxford: Basil Blackwell, 1987), pp. 140–53.

by some of which indeed the words may often be replaced" (*Einstellung*, p. 142). And if we follow this advice to situate the utterance in a context, it becomes clear that in this discussion Wittgenstein, although rejecting the picture of inward content behind the outward utterance, does not adopt the behaviorism that is the polemical antithesis to that dualistic picture. As Winch puts it, "Wittgenstein's rejection of this does not take the form of insisting that all he believes is that the other person is behaving in a certain way. His belief concerns someone to whom he has '*eine Einstellung zur Seele*' and this helps to make his belief what it is" (p. 142). And then, going on to what is for present concerns the most signficant remark in that essay, "We might say that what Wittgenstein is really protesting against in Section 310 is a sort of *impatience*."

Indeed, the desire to reduce and to encapsulate is far from unfamiliar in both linguistic and aesthetic analysis, and reductive encapsulation seems further endorsed by our sense of familiarity with these subjects. Thus Winch continues, "We are so familiar with the sort of behaviour and expressive demeanours that go with typical human feelings and emotions and with the expressive *responses* to such behaviour on the part of others, that we think we have a firm grasp of it and do not stop to look properly at it" ("*Einstellung*," p. 142). Indeed, the close readings I have attempted to sustain in the previous sections of this chapter and its predecessor are efforts at sustaining a kind of aesthetic patience, the reward of which is—and this will be discussed at length in Chapter 5—a sense of the complexities, of the subtleties, in short, an overview, that would remain unavailable to any more cursory or generalized interpretative method. Giving his articulation to some of the significance of Wittgenstein's densely compressed remark in the discussion in *Philosophical Investigations*, "His attitude is a proof of his attitude," Winch says this "means 'Just stop and look at what his attitude does actually consist in, perhaps you will be surprised at the subtleties and complexities involved; and when you have noticed them perhaps you will be less inclined to suppose that their significance must depend on something below the surface of which they are merely symptoms'." If, indeed, the attitude *is* proof of the attitude, then that is precisely what we should look at in detail, where the acts of looking are constantly mindful of the danger of reducing the subject to what we mistakenly take to be its true essence. Is the attitude, then, that we hold toward another human being really just a belief, or a set of beliefs, about that person as person? This formulation of the question is as erroneous as its affirmative answer. Is the attitude then a matter of certainty—beyond belief? This too, as we have seen, opens into error. The attitude is, again, the attitude, and if we want to see it then we have to look at it, and not at a reductive misconstrual of it. And again, this *kind* of looking is something that literature gives us more often than philosophy; it is thus no surprise that at this point in his essay Winch turns to a passage from Elizabeth Bowen's *Death of the Heart*, which includes the lines "Had the agitation she felt throughout her body sent out an aura with a quivering edge, Portia's eyes might be said to explore this line of quiver, round and along Anna's reclining form. Anna felt bound up with her fear, with her secret, by that enwrapping look of Portia's: she felt mummified. So she raised her voice when she said what time it was." This passage not only shows how thought, quite beyond the traditional dualistic picture of thinking standing behind speaking in one-to-one correlations, actually does stand behind speech; it also gives us something to look at patiently where "the physical interaction between Anna and Portia is, and is regarded as, what it is only within a complex web of human relationships" ("*Einstellung*," pp. 143–44). And then, having followed his own advice of having looked at the attitude to understand the attitude, and having more generally followed Wittgenstein's advice to "look and see" (and these are two instructions, not one), Winch is positioned to say, "It is a feature of such relationships that those who are involved in them have to each other *eine Einstellung zur Seele*."

Does there exist, however, and despite these recommendations to just look, a way of *generally* characterizing the attitude? If it is to serve as a model for our attitude to works of art, if this similar usage of "attitude" is endorsed by the multifarious analogies and commonalities between our perception of persons and of works of art already considered at length, ought we not to say something succinctly descriptive, something even elegantly concise, about this attitude?[14] Moving to a gestural metaphor, we might say that the attitude is a distinctive *stance* we take: but we would then have as quickly to add that it is not *really* a stance we *take*, since it is given in our form of life and is not subject to the will, and that it is, moreover, as a metaphor, something *like*, but not identical to, the attentiveness and state of receptivity indicated by the particular physical stance we might here envision (as a choreographer might envision it to signify attentiveness) as being appropriate to the attitude. But having only introduced the notion of a stance, we have already added detail well beyond what a stance implies and, more important, given the very notion of the stance content by referring back to the attitude. These are fairly clear symptoms that the attitude under discussion here is primitive, that it is indeed part of our natural history, and that it will, as such, resist formulaic or reductive encapsulation.[15] We may indeed be in pursuit of

---

14. See Wittgenstein's discussion in *The Blue and Brown Books* (Oxford: Basil Blackwell, 1958), pp. 17–19, in which we find the parenthetical remark on philosophical method: "Elegance is *not* what we are trying for."

15. In this connection, see Jerrold Levinson's deservedly much-discussed definition of the concept "Art" in "Defining Art Historically," in *Music, Art & Metaphysics* (Ithaca: Cornell University Press, 1990): "My idea is roughly this: a work of art is a thing intended for regard-as-a-work-of-art, regard in any of the ways works of art existing prior to it have been correctly regarded" (p. 6). Note that Levinson admirably avoids, without lapsing into vacuity or circularity, "analyzing art completely in nonart terms" (p. 6), and carefully preserves something very much like the (logically) primitive attitude I am discussing here as it manifests itself in both the perception of persons and of works of art. For a brief discussion of Levinson's definition, see my review of *Music, Art & Metaphysics* in *Canadian Philosophical Reviews* (forthcoming).

a human phenomenon that, although visible (if we are inclined to look in the right direction with the requisite patience), resists articulation where such articulation necessitates generalization. But this does not mean, of course, that we do not *know* this phenomenon—indeed there is nothing in this context epistemologically illegitimate about saying that we know it when we see it. It is thus no surprise, in Winch's essay, that a passage rendering this attitude crystalline is again quoted at length, this time from Simone Weil (which bears full reproduction here): "The human beings around us exert just by their presence a power which belongs uniquely to themselves to stop, to diminish, or modify, each movement which our bodies design. A person who crosses our path does not turn aside our steps in the same manner as a street sign, no one stands up, or moves about, or sits down in quite the same fashion when he is alone in a room as when he has a visitor."[16] Winch identifies as the crucial phrase in this passage "just by their presence," a passage that stands at once against an excessively ratiocinative analysis of the attitude—where the attitude is subsequent to a theory we hold about the source of the behavior before us—and against the temptation to attempt to translate this natural attitude to a person's presence into some formulation that leaves out a reference to, indeed, a *person's presence*.[17]

---

16. "*Eine Einstellung zur Seele*," p. 146. As a way of further elucidating the unmediated or nonratiocinative nature of our engagement with the aesthetic, consider a distinction drawn elsewhere by Winch concerning the understanding of morality: "Notice first that morality cannot be called, in the same sense as can science, a 'form of activity'; it is not something one can choose to engage in or not at will. It would hardly make sense, for instance, for someone to say he had spent six weeks working hard at morality (unless this meant something like moral *philosophy*), though it would be perfectly in order for him to say he had spent the time working hard at science" ("Nature and Convention," in *Ethics and Action* [London: Routledge & Kegan Paul, 1972], p. 58). I suggest that our participation in art, its role in our lives and its place in a culture, is far more like morality described here than like science.

17. Further against the desire to capture the attitude generally, Winch observes that *zur*, a contraction of the preposition *zu* and the definite article

Thus, as in the discussion of language in Chapters 1 and 2, we have again arrived at a level of phenomena where, as a part of our natural history, as a part of our form of life, and—in this case—as part of the web of human relationships and interactions, the instinctual and the irreducible enforce the patience that our swiftly moving theoretical desires would preclude.[18] And if it is true, as I have been arguing in the form of detailed literary interpretation, that the perception and understanding of a human being provides a useful model for our perception and understanding of works of art, that, as we might now put it, the attitude we find displayed as the fact of the moral case in a person's presence is, strikingly like, because it is deeply analogous to,[19] the attitude we find as the fact of the aesthetic case in the prescence of a work of art, then we ought not to be surprised at a perfectly parallel irreducibility.

---

der, suggests a connection between *Einstellung* and *Seele* in such a way that the concept of *Seele* is *necessary* to the characterization of the *Einstellung;* see "*Eine Einstellung zur Seele,*" p. 147. Although this runs rather quickly well beyond where I want to take it, it might be said that Dickie's famous failure to capture the aesthetic attitude is, after all, an attempt to capture the attitude as it is willfully adopted in isolation from its object, and it is thus no wonder that he failed. See especially Dickie, "The Myth of the Aesthetic Attitude," in Hospers, ed., *Introductory Readings in Aesthetics.*

18. These desires generate a syllogism that Winch carefully avoids. He says, of our response to, for example, someone's being given news of the death of someone he loves, "How he will suffer," that this is *not* the result of "All men suffer at such news; This man is having such news; Therefore...." That ratiocinative reconstruction is, as Winch identifies it, "mythological"; beyond this it might be added that this characterization of our response, as something approximating a computer simulation of the sympathetic imagination, is utterly inhuman. It might also be mentioned that, because of the pretheoretical or preratiocinative "stance" or attitude we hold—like our attitudes toward persons—we are perhaps closer to the cave painters than we know.

19. I use the metaphor of depth again to indicate that the understanding of the arts in a culture will be as *rooted* in natural human practices as is the understanding of persons.

Aspects of Interpretation 139

"THE FIGURE IN THE CARPET"

"The Figure in the Carpet" is a tale of reductionism versus antireductionism and, ultimately, impatience versus patience. And like a small "machine to think with," this story not only depicts the desire to reduce and encapsulate, but provides its readers an opportunity to reflect on that desire by masterfully inducing it in them.

The story begins with a young writer reflecting on his opportunity to review Hugh Vereker's new novel and his opportunity to meet the author the following Sunday. The review will appear in the literary journal *The Middle*, which is indeed the intermediary between the work of fiction itself and that work's reading public. A more experienced critic, Corvick, has promised to review Vereker's latest book, but cannot now fulfill that promise because he has been called away to Paris. Before departing, however, Corvick sets up the critical puzzle for the younger man: "For God's sake try to get *at* him ... Speak of him, you know, if you can, as *I* should have spoken of him."[20] Our narrator-critic misunderstands immediately, and making the wrong move in the puzzle (and thus giving the puzzle greater definition): "You mean as far and away the biggest of the lot—that sort of thing?" Telling him not to put authors "back to back" in that way, Corvick refers instead to an unnamed quality of Vereker's work: " 'But he gives me a pleasure so rare; the sense of'—he mused a little—'something or other'." The critical puzzle is thus established, and confirmed with the exchange " 'The sense, pray, of what?' 'My dear man, that's just what I want *you* to say!' " And he sits up half the night, reading Vereker, congratulating himself on having grown beyond the critical "infancy" of just saying who

---

20. Henry James, "The Figure in the Carpet," in *The Figure in the Carpet and Other Stories*, pp. 358–59.

is better without saying why, and trying to fill in the interpretative gap that Corvick has opened.

On Sunday morning our critic is contemplating Vereker from a distance, feeling sure that he hasn't yet read the review that has appeared in the interim in *The Middle*. But a certain Lady Jane appears, brandishing a copy, telling Vereker he must read this man (not now knowing the critic is in her company) who has "got at you, at what *I* always feel, you know" (p. 361). Later, at the table, Miss Poyle, the vicar's sister, asks Vereker directly what he thinks of the review (having just read it upstairs) so highly praised by Lady Jane, and he replies, neither of them aware that the author is beside them, "Oh it's all right—the usual twaddle!" Advancing his critical search, Poyle asks, "You mean he doesn't do you justice?" and he replies, evasively, "It's a charming article." But then the unnamed critical or interpretative vision is further surrounded: " 'All I pretend is that the author doesn't see' "—" 'Doesn't see what?' " ... " 'Doesn't see anything.' " " 'Dear me—how very stupid!' " And then, concluding the exchange and in so doing signing and sealing the interpretative orders that our young critic is receiving: " 'Not a bit', Vereker laughed again. 'Nobody does'."

Having avoided Vereker after dinner and feeling rather dejected, our critic nevertheless encounters him, who apologizes for having "unwittingly wounded" him, having of course learned his identity. In the extended conversation to follow, we learn that Vereker feels as misunderstood by favorable reviews as by unfavorable, that they always "miss his little point," and that, when asked directly what this point is, he replies, "Have I got to *tell* you, after all these years and labours?" (p. 365). This remark itself suggests that not only has his point been missed, but that it is the sort of point that has taken, not a short paragraph, but "years and labours." Our critic misses this implication—he is by no means yet the sort of reader on whom nothing is lost—and he only becomes more determined to uncover *a* point. Vereker says that the point is what he has written all this work *for*, the part of his art where "the flame of art burns most intensely." Our critic, peering into the haze of these generalities about aesthetic motivation, says in a way that reveals his increasing insistence on critical and unitary encapsulation, "Your description's certainly beautiful, but it doesn't make what you describe very distinct." What Vereker is describing, as we shall see, may not be very distinct, and it would thus be only misrepresentation, misconstrual, to render it that way. Indeed, if Vereker is the artist we here see him to be, he would be extraordinarily sensitive to the aesthetic failure of reductive oversimplification. This is a sensitivity our critic not only cannot yet feel; he cannot yet imagine it. Further into this conversation he is given reason to doubt his formulaic method: "You call it a little trick?" he asks Vereker, and the reply makes a move toward indicating the scope of the critical method he will need, "That's only my little modesty. It's really an exquisite scheme" (p. 366). And almost telling him that the "secret" is in the writing itself and not in a hidden unitary reduction behind it, in response to the question "Don't you think you ought— just a trifle—to assist the critic?" Vereker asks "Assist him? What else have I done with every stroke of my pen?" Not all tautologies are redundant,[21] and one is tempted here, as a reader sympathetic to Vereker, to turn to the critic and say slowly and carefully, " 'Every stroke of the pen' *means* 'Every stroke of the pen.' " But Vereker knows the gripping temptation of encapsulation and of the contemptuous attitude toward the particular work of fiction so encapsulated which yielding to this temptation engenders; he adds, "I've shouted my intention in his great blank face." And he says of his "great affair" (again challenging the conception of critical summary presumed by our narrator) that *is* his secret that it is "a secret in spite of itself." This description, for its accuracy, requires that the "secret" be plainly

---

21. Another example is Wittgenstein's remark above that the attitude *is* the evidence for the attitude.

visible—if one knows where, and how, that is, patiently, to look. But burning with interpretative desire ("You fire me as I've never been fired"), this critic only queries, "Is it a kind of esoteric message?" With gestures again conveying significance that our narrator cannot really comprehend, "His [Vereker's] countenance fell at this—he put out his hand as if to bid me good night." But at this juncture Vereker adds as well; "Ah my dear fellow, it can't be described in cheap journalese!" (p. 367).

Predictably, our critic won't quit, and he soon elicits from Vereker the further explanation: "My whole lucid effort gives him the clue—every page and line and letter. The thing's as concrete there as a bird in a cage, a bait on a hook, a piece of cheese in a mousetrap. It's stuck into every volume as your foot is stuck into your shoe. It governs every line, it chooses every word, it dots every i, it places every comma." Again, a reader might feel a desire to intercede on Vereker's behalf, again reciting to the critic a string of what in this context again become nonredundant tautologies; "whole" means "whole"; "every" means "every"; "concrete" means "concrete"; and so on. This is, however, not exactly accurate; a *re*-reader might feel this desire. At first—and here James is placing his reader in precisely the epistemological position of the narrator-critic—it is difficult not to sympathize with his critical search for the unitary encapsulation of literary meaning, to feel this temptation along with him, even if we find his formulation of this temptation objectionable. Scratching his head and introducing familiar critical categories, our critic asks if it is then "something in the style or something in the thought? An element of form or an element of feeling?" But he is not incapable of ascending beyond this infantile aesthetic, for a moment later—a moment in which Vereker has again replaced speech with gesture and simply again shaken his hand—he "felt his questions to be crude and [his] distinctions pitiful." And he ascends still higher, asking if "it's some sort of idea *about* life, some sort of philosophy," but for this critical ascent falls all the harder, venturing that perhaps its "some kind of game . . . some-

Aspects of Interpretation 143

thing you're after in the language. Perhaps it's a preference for the letter P! ... Papa, potatoes, prunes ... that sort of thing." It is clear that a repetition in this case of his own words *in the language* would fail to perform the function they might. In search of "the secret," he is in critical oblivion.

This desire makes it impossible for him to enjoy Vereker's fiction: "I not only failed to run a general intention to earth, I found myself missing the subordinate intentions I had formerly enjoyed" (p. 370). James having here recorded the deadening and desensitizing influence of the superimposition of a generalized critical method, our narrator next embraces interpretative skepticism over this absence of the secret, the essence of Vereker's work: "I *had* no knowledge—nobody had any." Here patiently looking and seeing, looking into the works themselves, appears as remote a possibility as it was in the attempt to generally characterize the attitude to which Wittgenstein objected above; and it is, here too somewhat ironically, the very presumption of great familiarity that eases the move into skepticism. And as our critic gazes across the gulf separating ignorance from knowledge, he imagines that knowledge to be "something... in the primal plan; something like a complex figure in a Persian carpet." Much later, he is in part reconciled to his ignorance, but still "deep down ... uneasy," still in a "disconcerted state—for [his] wonted curiosity lived in its ashes" (p. 376). This picture of literary meaning has its grip, and in him that grip is not easily loosened. And here too the aesthetic has repercussions in the ethical, the powerful grip making marks on art and on life: "Not only had I lost the books, but I had lost the man himself: they and their author had been alike spoiled for me."

Over time the critical secret assumes the status of epistemological "buried treasure" (p. 380), but little by little curiosity began "to ache again"—where James has again shown that the emotive and the cognitive are not always disparate, as in this case in which he captures the *feeling* of a focused ignorance—which becomes, indeed, "torment." It is in this state that he learns of a cable from Corvick in Bombay, who sends "Eureka. Immense"—and nothing more. The recipient of this telegram, Gwendolen Erme, tells our critic that the secret itself, let alone for six months, has "sprung out at him like a tigress out of the jungle" and that they (every page of Vereker's work) "all worked in him together... and when he wasn't thinking, they fell, in all their superb intricacy, into the one right combination." It would be too deliberate a philosophical projection onto these words to say that they illustrate the practice Wittgenstein recommended of stopping thinking and *looking* instead, but not too much to say that there is here a kind of recipe for legitimate critical enlightenment of the sort Corvick has apparently achieved: "Every" page... worked in him together." And indeed Corvick's travel was designed to produce "the difference of thought," a different way of thinking critically—perhaps a way free of the blinding limitations of an essence-presuming encapsulating method—that "would give the needed touch." And she adds, most suggestively, "Perhaps it can't be got into a letter if it's 'immense'." But failing to allow even the possibility of thinking in a new, nonreductive way, our critic fails to see that it can be epistemologically legitimate to say *that* one has seen something of "immense" significance without being able to say, in succinct form, *what* that seeing was of. And indeed, if it is a kind of overview (of the sort we will examine directly in the next chapter), one of the things one thereby knows as a function of that overview is in fact *not* to try to encapsulate. He thus says, "Perhaps not if it's immense bosh. If he had hold of something that can't be got into a letter he hasn't got hold of *the* thing." With an air that is recognizably Jamesian, Corvick returns, marries Gwendolen, begins the process of writing the critical work on Vereker that will "trace the figure in the carpet through every convolution, to reproduce it in every tint" (p. 387), itself a description fighting against reductionism. But on a whim Corvick takes his young bride for a drive and, in an accident, is "killed on the spot; Gwendolen escaped unhurt." With this direct avenue into critical knowledge closed, our narrator later pursues the indirect, asking Gwendolen about the manuscript in progress, only to learn that it is a "mere heartbreaking scrap." And with the few manuscript pages revealing nothing, he then naturally wants to know: "Had *she* seen the idol unveiled?" Driven by the desire for interpretative essence, he asks, only to learn, "I heard everything... and I mean to keep it to myself!" Indeed, if he were paying attention, if he could see from within the confines of his essentialist strategy the significance of detail, and if he had the patience such a strategy brusquely dismisses, he would notice that she heard, not *the* thing, not *the* secret, not *a* key, but *every*thing.

Later still, while sitting with Mrs. Corvick one evening, he puts it directly: "Now at last what *is* it?" (p. 392). And in a one-word response requiring a lengthy description to convey its meaning ("the largest finest coldest 'Never!' I had yet, in the course of a life that had known denials, had to take full in the face"), she begins to show not that she will not, but that she cannot, tell him—thus beginning to draw again the distinction between what one can "see" and what one can, directly, say. In a shamefully desperate ploy he says, "I know what to think then. It's nothing." With a "remote disdainful pity" that he sees in her "dim smile," she says, speaking in a tone of voice that our narrator makes it clear he will not forget, and where that tone indicates a vast unarticulated significance, "It's my *life*!"

All of this weighs against reductionism, against the possibility of succinctly or propositionally encapsulating meaning, and moreover the utterance "It's my life!" itself carries, within this context in which tone, gesture, history, and what we know about the mind of the hearer as well as the speaker all shape the vast *and* unarticulated significance of the utterance. And showing the moral repercussion of this epistemological limit and the feverish and reckless desire to overcome it, she adds, "You've insulted him!" From the depths of incomprehension he asks, "Do you mean Vereker?" With what we must hear as a pained utterance, she answers, "I mean the Dead!" Among the things she sees that she cannot here say—because such an observation would be lost on our determined critic burdened by an impoverished conception particularly of literary meaning and more generally of the scope of linguistic significance—is the fact that the very formulation of the question he put, with its presumed unitary answer, insults the achievement of the Dead because it fails to acknowledge even the possibility of a hard-won epistemological station. It epistemologically cheapens and, in this context, simultaneously morally offends.

Toward the end of this story Vereker dies, followed shortly by his wife, another source that might have been approached "with the feeble flicker of my plea," as our narrator now puts it. With these sources closed, he now takes the short step from critical scepticism to epistemological solipsism: "I was shut up in my obsession for ever—my gaolers had gone off with the key" (p. 395). But then Mrs. Corvick marries a certain Drayton Deane, also a critic but one who has never, to the frustration of our narrator, written on Vereker. Later still, she dies, leaving Deane for the final encounter with our narrator. The words he utters at this meeting convey a great deal more about his now utterly debased conception of literary content than he realizes, calling the long-pursued secret "information." "I shall be glad to make any terms that you see fit to name for the information she must have had from George Corvick." This is the language of the exchange of commodities, and that commodity is here pictured, in a profoundly erroneous way, as a unitary, simple, and stable piece of information. But, after discussion, it becomes clear that Deane truthfully does not know what is being talked about. Our narrator says, in response to Deane's remark, that if there had been such knowledge she would have wanted it used (reinforcing the language of commodity exchange), and our narrator replies, with words he does not and cannot understand, "It *was* used. She used it herself. She told me with her own lips that she 'lived' on it." Indeed, if the secret is that literature is *itself* a source of knowledge, and if she came to realize—in a way that cannot be bought or sold, nor communicated in the form of declarative propositions—that what she can see in the world, the aspects, characteristics, qualities, and interconnections between persons and things, can be expanded and given shape and coherence by what she sees in literature that answers to a higher mimetic calling,[22] then she *could* have "lived" on it; that is, everything

22. See my "Aristotle's *Mimesis* and Abstract Art," *Philosophy* 59 (July 1984): 365–71, for a brief discussion of the meaning of "mimesis" as I employ the term. On construing the "secret" developed above, one might recall James's remark concerning the power of art: "It is art that *makes* life, makes interest, makes importance, for our consideration and application of these things, and I know of no substitute whatever for the force and beauty of its process." (See Kermode's introduction to James, *The Figure in the Carpet*, p. 11.) Moreover, James asserts that "the province of art is all life (p. 10). In connection with my suggestion that the "secret" is irreducible, see Kermode's remark that when "James speaks of the 'intention' of his work, he is not suggesting that there is some simply apprehensible design to which correct interpretation must exactly conform" (p. 26). George Watson has said of "The Figure in the Carpet" that "it is important to recognize that the ironic force of the story lies not, as some critics have supposed, in any assumption that Vereker's secret is not worth having—but in the narrator's single-minded attempt to discover the novelist's secret in any way except by a careful reading of the novels. Each interview takes him further away from the intelligence of the dead genius—where a 'close or analytic appreciation' might have led him straight to the secret" (*The LiteraryCritics* [London: Hogarth, 1986], p. 156). F. R. Leavis has said of James's "handling of the theme of morality," that it "covers more than one issue" and that within a single text we often find "a shifting force" ("James as Critic," in *The Critic as Anti-Philosopher*, ed. G. Singh [London: Chatto & Windus, 1982], pp. 112–13). Of course close, patient, and analytical readings are prerequisites for an appreciation of the significance of Leavis's remark. Where "philosophical" means "essentialistic," this is most certainly "antiphilosophical." (I will discuss the philosophical method of essentialism directly in Chapter 5.) Last, it should be said that the theme of the misunderstood Master, frustrated by impatient and thus uncomprehending criticism, is familiar in James, and indeed *his* "secret"—mimetic fidelity of a higher sort, realism, a mimesis that takes all of life and all reflection on that life as its proper subject—is manifested throughout his writings. (See Lionel Trilling's remark in *The Liberal Imagination*,

within the limits of her perceptual world could have been enlivened by it. It may, indeed, have been a *vision* of the scope of literature—where that scope is continually expanded through reflection on what is contained within it—and of the *significance* of critical activity that Corvick achieved in Bombay and that he found "immense," the dimension of the literary world that contributes to that vision.

"The Figure in the Carpet" is a cautionary tale, a story that shows us how a narrow propositional monism elevated to an interpretative methodology can blind one epistemologically and morally, how it is intrinsically futile to attempt to deliver *the* meaning of something as complicated, as lifelike, as a literary work. To look, impatiently, at a life and try to state succinctly in a factual assertion its meaning would be *prima facie* ludicrous. And although it is not an entirely obvious matter, to try to define succinctly the exact nature of the "primitive" attitude we hold toward that life is, as we saw in the first part of this section, equally unacceptable. Thus the analogy that we have been considering throughout between works of art and persons is given further specified content here, for the attempt to state literary meaning in a unitary form, and the attempt to define succinctly our attitude toward that fictional work in engaging with it in such a way that it "enlivens," equally lead us to look impatiently in the wrong direction. James has here in fact given us good reason to think that the distinction between philosophy as an analytical activity and philosophy as an interpretative or literary-critical activity might well be illusory. But James as well as Wittgenstein has now heightened our sensitivity to the fact that some things are better shown than said and that what one sees from an overview is not something one can say succinctly.

p. 70: "The social texture of his work is grainy and knotted with practicality and detail.") In Chapter 1 and 2 we saw something of the reasons for Wittgenstein's struggle with his own earlier "unifying" work; James is, in a way, conducting in his writing a parallel struggle against essentialism, employing in the struggle what is for him a kind of literary fail-safe: an honest mimesis.

5

~ Interpretation and Philosophical Method

It is clear that Wittgenstein, in his later philosophy, brought a deep and powerful argument against a certain conception of philosophical activity, and that this argument was startlingly revolutionary in both content and method. He cast his argument in the form of a philosophical investigation;[1] the old conception of philosophy, which his supplanted, was that of a conceptual analysis in search of an essence. The implications of Wittgenstein's position have of course been discussed, both for philosophy in general and for aesthetic theory in particular, but only in one direction[2]—from Wittgenstein's position to the concept of art, culminating in the familiar conclusion that art is not a unitary concept, that there is no single essential feature both necessary and sufficient for the classification of an object

---

1. One might with greater accuracy say that Wittgenstein provided the directions for the investigation; his later writings deliberately leave a great deal of work to the reader.

2. See Renford Bambrough, "Universals and Family Resemblances," *Proceedings of the Aristotelian Society* 61 (1960–61): 207–22; reprinted in *Wittgenstein: The Philosophical Investigations*, ed. George Pitcher (New York: Macmillan, 1966). See also Morris Weitz, "The Role of Theory in Aesthetics," *Journal of Aesthetics and Art Criticism* 15 (Fall 1957): 27–35, and "Wittgenstein's Aesthetics," in *Language and Aesthetics*, ed. B. R. Tilghman (Lawrence: University of Kansas Press, 1973).

as a work of art. In this final chapter I want to reverse this direction and ask what significance art, particularly fiction, can hold for our conception of philosophy. Specifically, I argue that we can indeed arrive at a deeper comprehension of the Wittgensteinian philosophical investigation through closely examining a piece of fiction than through any attempt to summarize his method in metaphilosophical terms.

If we begin by asking the question that some might claim lies at the center of philosophy, "What is knowledge?" we will, if bound by the essentialist presumption, search for a feature, an element, an attribute, indeed an *essence*, that is present in every case of knowledge and that by virtue of its presence, renders the case in question a case of knowledge. Thus just as scotch is identified as a member of a certain class of beverages by virtue of the presence of a certain distillate, so cases of knowledge are on this traditional view thought to be made to be what they are, to count as knowledge, through the presence of some common ingredient. This definitional core of the concept of knowledge has been given many formulations; perhaps the most prominent has been that of justified true belief.[3]

This essentialist presumption is the position against which Wittgenstein's argument was posed. Should we not at this point ask for a sketch of Wittgenstein's position? Consider Wittgenstein's own words: "I cannot characterize my standpoint better than by saying that it is opposed to that which Socrates represents in the Platonic dialogues. For if asked what knowledge is I would list examples of knowledge, and add the words 'and the like'. No common element is to be found in them all."[4] This,

---

3. The fundamental defense of the view of knowledge as justified true belief is in Plato, *Theaetetus* 201 and *Meno* 98. See also A. J. Ayer, *The Problem of Knowledge* (New York: Macmillan, 1956), p. 34, and E. L. Gettier, "Is Justified True Belief Knowledge?" *Analysis* 23 (1963): 121–23, reprinted in *Knowledge and Belief*, ed. A. P. Griffiths (Oxford: Oxford University Press, 1967).

4. This passage is quoted from the unpublished manuscripts in Garth Hal-

as a sketch of a position, is undeniably disappointing. It tells us, again, what the argument is *opposed* to; it does not shed much light on the actual argument or the new method of investigation. But this is not surprising, for a well-known aspect of Wittgenstein's later philosophy is the initially somewhat mysterious impossibility of encapsulating or, indeed, of generally characterizing the standpoint. What, we want to know with some precision, *is* a philosophical investigation, and how exactly is such an investigation significant for aesthetic interpretation? To answer this question we turn once again to literature.

"THE TREE OF KNOWLEDGE"

From James's characteristically compressed short story "The Tree of Knowledge,"[5] one can derive an expansive list of the varieties of knowledge. The story itself is constructed around four characters, a father and mother, their son, and a friend of the family. But, not surprisingly, there ends the simplicity. The father is a sculptor, known by the family as "the Master"; his name to the world beyond this slightly extended family circle is Morgan Mallow. Mrs. Mallow is a gentle soul who "rejoices" in her husband's statues, and she is "attached to (the friend) Peter Brench...because of his affection for Morgan." Peter Brench, however, even though sincerely good friends with Morgan, has secretly been in love with Mrs. Mallow for years. Although all know that Peter has reached the age of fifty and "escaped marriage," they do not know precisely how he has managed this. Furthermore, James, as the narrator, tells us in

---

lett, *A Companion to Wittgenstein's* Philosophical Investigations (Ithaca: Cornell University Press, 1977), p. 33.

5. Henry James, "The Tree of Knowledge," in *The Short Stories of Henry James*, ed. Clifton Fadiman (New York: Random House, 1945). As this is indeed a very short story I have in this case omitted specific page references.

the opening lines of the story that "it was one of the secret opinions, such as we all have, of Peter Brench that his main success in life would have consisted in his never having committed himself about the work, as it was called, of his friend Morgan Mallow." It was "nowhere on record that he had... either lied or spoken the truth." Thus Brench's private distaste for Morgan's work is only equaled in strength by his equally private affection for Morgan's wife. But although he conceals his feelings for the work and the wife, he neither conceals nor needs to pretend a sincere affection for Morgan, which exists in spite of what for many would be rather serious obstacles. The narrator tells us that "it became thus a real wonder that the friends in whom he had most confidence were just those with whom he has most reserves." Lancelot, the son, had gone up to Cambridge when he was nineteen and had come down again when he was twenty, and it was concluded, against the great efforts and protestations of Peter, that Lance, with his deep if not particularly old heritage, had simply been born, not to the book, but to the brush. So, despite Peter's suggestions that Lance just stay at home (at Peter's expense), or that he go back again to Peter's old college (again at Peter's expense, this time both financially and socially), off Lance goes to Paris. And, as we shall see, Lance returns full of knowledge about himself, about his father, through this learns about his mother, and inadvertently and most interestingly changes Peter's relationship to the truth. But we must, before considering this epistemological evolution, now return to the categories of knowledge.[6]

There are, of course, those things we know which we both know to be true of ourselves and which we naturally and openly reveal. For example, Morgan regards himself as an artist (and

---

6. This list is not complete, nor are the boundaries between the members of it as distinct as perhaps they could be. I intend this list to serve as a secure place from which to begin an exploration of the significance of "The Tree of Knowledge" for our conception of knowledge.

a great one at that), and it is clear to Morgan, from, as one might say, the inside, and to all others, from the outside, that this is true. Other perfectly obvious examples of this first category are readily available: Mr. and Mrs. Mallow are married to each other and regard themselves as being so; they have a son named Lance who in turn regards himself as their son, and so on.[7] This is, as I said, a perfectly unproblematic category; that is, it does not of itself generate any particular puzzlement concerning the nature of knowledge.

The second category is only slightly more complicated: there are things we know to be true of ourselves but which we do not reveal openly. Peter knows all too well that he is, and has been for years, in love with Mrs. Mallow. Peter, however, is the only one to know this. Using the terms introduced above we might say that he knows this from the inside but that no one else know it, indeed that it cannot under present conditions be known, from the outside. We see this in the text in a discussion between Peter and Mrs. Mallow concerning Lance's future, in which she asks whether or not Peter believes that Lance possesses the gift of the Master, the passion to create. After confessing that he had noticed a certain disposition on the part of the boy "to daub and draw" he reports that he had "hoped it would burn out." She replies, "But why should it...with his wonderful heredity? Passion is passion—though of course *you*, dear Peter, know nothing of that." Here only Peter knows, from the first-person case,[8] how far from the truth this is; from the outside, that is, judging from purely outward or behavioral

---

7. Some would argue that these are not cases of knowledge because they are too obvious to be mentioned as such. I will not discuss the problem of the "assertion fallacy" here. See John Searle, *Speech Acts* (Cambridge: Cambridge University Press, 1969), pp. 141–45. I leave it to the reader to imagine cases in which we would say that Mr. and Mrs. Mallow are married, they have a son Lance, etc.

8. I use the phrase "first-person case" cautiously; I do not mean to imply that Peter *learned* the concept of love through acts of inner ostensive definition.

criteria, it is an eminently reasonable belief, one which in fact would seem to all to be *obviously* true, as in the first category of knowledge.

The next category is filled by those things we do not know of ourselves but which others do, which is simply a reversal of the previous category. And Lance, it appears, very neatly exemplifies this type. He knows that he is failing as a student, and with the mounting evidence, "It had been impossible longer to remain blind to the fact that he was gaining no glory" at his college; that is, the external evidence finally forced the realization on his parents. He is, then, searching for a new future, and considers going to Paris, the place of choice to develop his inborn talent. In discussing the matter with Peter he says, "One has got, today... don't you see, to know," here referring to the need to authentically sound one's own depths, to know one's own abilities and to enjoy a certain security in that self-knowledge; in short, one must have the security of being, he says, properly situated in life. But Peter, who will by now have been recognized as something of the visionary concerning art and talent, already knows that the boy is simply no good at painting. He is in a position to see that this is the case, as anyone with any perspective that runs beyond the Master's fabric of self-deception would know. James has captured here an important distinction: Lance honestly does not yet know his own worth, and it is not something of which we can say he *ought* to know, precisely because he has not been given the kind of perspective from which it would all be rather painfully obvious. So Lance does not know a fact about himself, another (Peter) does know, and it is not—at least not yet—the case that he ought to know. One characteristic of this category of knowledge is that the one who does know can tell us, perhaps rightly, that we are better off not knowing. And this is, in fact, precisely what Peter does say to the young man: "Oh hang it, *don't* know! ... It isn't knowledge, it's ignorance that—as we've been beautifully told—is bliss."

The next category, the fourth, is similar to the previous in that we do not know something about ourselves and others do, except that here it can be said of us that we ought to know. In this case it is only through the preservation of some elaborate web of self-deception that we manage to escape the unwanted truth. This category is perfectly illustrated by Morgan, whose defense mechanisms against the facts are spelled out by James with considerable clarity. We already know that he is referred to as "the Master," but only by the family group. And we learn that, in what have been succinctly called "belief-adverse" circumstances,[9] Morgan had "everything of the sculptor but the spirit of Phidias," that is, all the trappings but none of the talent. He had "the brown velvet, the becoming *beretto*, the 'plastic' presence, the fine fingers, the beautiful accent in Italian and the old Italian factotum." The illusion was all the easier to sustain, Mrs. Mallow "having brought him in marriage a portion that put them in a manner at their ease and enabled them thus... to keep it up." Thus "Carerra Lodge," as it was called, was not supported by carved marble but by inheritance. This prosperity also made it all the easier to attribute Morgan's failure to sell a single work, to win a single award, to gain any variety of external recognition whatsoever, to the tastelessness of the uncomprehending masses. Speaking of Lance's future in the art world to Peter, Mrs. Mallow asks if Lance will "incur the jealousies and provoke the machinations that have been at times almost too much for his father?" She goes on to refer to the "claptrap" that one must produce in "these dreadful days," the "curse of refinement and distinction" for which Morgan has suffered, and the possibility that Lance too might "wing his flight further than the vulgar taste of his stupid countrymen." We are given all of these details, both about the personal style of the Master and these explanations of his lack of outward

9. See Herbert Fingarette, *Self-Deception* (London: Routledge & Kegan Paul, 1969), pp. 12–33.

forms of encouragement, in order that James might show us precisely how these individual strands of self-deception are interwoven and in the end how they, taken as a whole, constitute the veil that shields Morgan from himself. And the opaque density of that veil is indicated in the story by Morgan's regret that he had not been a painter instead—for he would like to have contributed to the great room at the Uffizi, the presumption being of course that the Uffizi would have been happy to acquire anything issuing from his masterly hand.

Morgan and Lance differ, then, in the self-knowledge we can reasonably expect of them. Lance does not, and especially in these circumstances could not, yet know his own abilities. Morgan, like Lance, does not know either, although he might well be expected to know, and there are indeed ways in which the very fact of his sustained act of self-deceit will render him blameworthy.[10] But the contrast between these two types of knowledge is marked in another way as well: in the case in which we do not know the fact about ourselves but ought to, we *could* learn this from the inside: that is, pure reflection on one's own case would, given sufficient seriousness and depth of thought, effect this discovery. In the other case, Lance's position, there is nothing to be learned from the inside. There are things we can *only* know from others; we might condense this point by saying that self-knowledge of this particular sort assumes other-knowledge.[11]

The fifth variety includes those things we know but wish we did not. It has been a commonplace at least since Oedipus that

---

10. Notice that in this as in so many detailed literary cases, the alleged gap traditionally said to exist between facts and values has been crossed before we are aware of its presence—rendering the very idea of the gap dubious.

11. That is, self-knowledge of this *particular* sort; I do not want here to deny the asymmetry that holds quite generally between self-knowledge and other-knowledge of the sort that has been discussed by John Wisdom in *Philosophy and Psycho-analysis* (Oxford: Basil Blackwell, 1953) and *Other Minds* (Oxford: Basil Blackwell, 1952). As is made clear in those discussions, it is by no means necessary to assimilate self- to other-knowledge to avoid solipsism.

Interpretation and Philosophical Method 157

knowledge and happiness are not always positively correlated; knowing things can burden us to the extent that we find ourselves longing for an earlier state of ignorance, before we were hurt by the truth. In such cases we can, of course, still very much want to know the truth and, not incompatibly, not want the truth we learn to be the case. Often of course we are placed in morally difficult situations because of what we know, and in these situation will agree that ignorance can be bliss. And this, we gradually come to see, is precisely Peter's position, and he is heard sounding warnings about the dangers of knowing throughout the story. We have already seen him issue one such warning to Lance. Next in that conversation Lance asks Peter if he thinks he possesses talent, and Peter replies, casually and elusively, "How do I know?" This feigning of ignorance stops when Lance says, "Oh, if it's your own ignorance you're defending—!" and Peter says, after a pause, "It isn't. I've the misfortune to be omniscient." The serious core of this joking remark is that in comparison to the others, he *is* omniscient. He knows what the Master's works are worth. He knows what his true feeling for Mrs. Mallow are. He knows what the real likelihood of Lance's possessing great artistic talent is. And he knows that this position of greater knowledge is a burden. Lance says, laughing, "Oh well, if you know *too* much—!" and Peter replies, in a way that at this point only he can understand, "That's what I do, and it's why I'm so wretched."

EPISTEMOLOGICAL FICTION

We now have a sense of the initial positions of the characters in "The Tree of Knowledge." We now must look closely at the text to follow their movements, or, to be more specific, their changing relationships to the truth.

We know that Peter is singularly sensitive to the dangers of knowledge. In disapproving of Paris, he says to Lance, "Well,

I'm afraid of it." "Ah, I see!" Lance replies, as though it is merely a matter of his elder fearing the unfamiliar. Peter shows that this is not a simple fear, however, by replying in turn, "No, you don't see—yet. But you will—that is you would. And you mustn't." "We're so safe," Peter says, "Come, don't spoil it." Lance begins to suspect that Peter's resistance somehow runs deeper, and, "Watching him with eyes that showed suspicion," accuses Peter of thinking that he lacks the requisite talent. Here James takes the opportunity to comment on the fragility of the happiness that rests on illusion: Peter says, "Well, what do you call success?" and Lance replies, "Why, the best sort, I suppose, is to please one's self. Isn't that the sort that, in spite of the cabals and things, is—in his own peculiar line—the Master's?" This question, the narrator tells us, is so heavily laden with complication that it has the understandable effect of freezing the conversation in its tracks. We learn that, although to have Lance believe in his father was "exactly what Peter... above all ...desired; yet perversely enough it gave him a chill." The chill is, of course, one result of the collision of appearance with reality. The tension between truth and illusion, at least at this stage, can only be felt by Peter. He knows, from one vantage point, that his desire is simply to preserve the illusion of the Master's qualities, and yet he also knows that far from being "the best sort of success," it is in truth among the worst forms of failure.

In a passage describing the Master's work James provides what can be interpreted as the visual analogue to this curious family whose sense of order and proportion is lost to the imbalances of knowledge:

> The creations that so failed to reveal it [the Master's artistic "idea"] stood about on pedestals and brackets, on tables and shelves, a little staring white population, heroic, idyllic, allegoric, mythic, symbolic, in which "scale" had so strayed and lost itself that the public square and chimney-piece seemed to have

changed places, the monumental being all diminutive and the diminutive all monumental; branches at any rate, markedly, of a family in which stature was rather oddly irrespective of function, age, and sex. They formed, like the Mallows themselves, poor Brench's own family.

Indeed, what the Master's collection, his "family" of works, seems to represent better than anything else through its disproportionate design and its "strayed scale," is the Master's own illusory world. Here art, if we can use the term loosely, actually does hold a mirror up not only to appearances but to reality.

James provides considerable insight into the inner structure of self-deception, showing how it is that we can, with the image of certainty, seem to know what is not the case. He tells us that it is Morgan's *mis*fortune occasionally to receive a commission for a work, which this time comes from a bereaved couple who desire a monument to their lost children. Each of these infrequent and always somewhat unusual commissions generate the belief that he would soon be swamped with requests, and they "eased the wound of elections never won, the long ache of medals and diplomas carried off, on every chance, by everyone but the Master; it moreover lighted the lamp that would glimmer through the next eclipse." Careful never to "prick the bubble in advance," Morgan is certain on each of these occasions that it will be the first in a well-deserved unending series. All of this is of course further supported by the view that "the Master was always too good to sell." James's theoretical point, interesting for its simultaneous simplicity and depth, is that belief, masquerading as knowledge, can survive, and indeed flourish, on very little encouragement; only a few shreds of charitably interpreted evidence are required to sustain it.

In further elucidating the characteristics of the category of things we ought to know but do not, James shows how delicate brushes with the truth can be accommodated, and a direct confrontation averted, through reinterpretation and rationalization. This is subtly shown by James when he has Peter say, in conversation with the Mallows, "I don't care what you may call it when a fellow doesn't—but Lance must learn to *sell*, you know. I drink to his acquisition of the secret of a base popularity!" James next makes Mrs. Mallow speak, who, as our narrator describes it, "rather artlessly allowed that *he* (Lance) must sell." But why is this remark artless? Failing to treat the knowledge with the delicacy it deserves in this context, this remark draws a stark and obvious contrast between the Master and those who sell, carrying a concealed but still pointed threat of cold truth. That it is in a less than fully conscious way taken as a threat is proven, not in the content, but in the timing, of the Master's response; " 'Ah', the sculptor after a moment confidently pronounced, Lance *will*. Don't be afraid. He'll have learnt." The moment was here taken while an alternative and less threatening formulation of the facts was produced by the Master, and the explanatory results of this illusion-sustaining reflection are indeed housed in the following passages. Mrs. Mallow quickly adds, "Which is exactly what Peter ... wouldn't when he told him hear of," suggesting that Peter's objections to Lance's becoming an artist are based not on a fear of utter failure but on a fear of commercialism. The fears thus imputed to Peter are then described by Morgan to be only the "French tricks," the impure artistic practices of the Continent, which erode artistic integrity but guarantee gallery sales. And James now shows us the result of this illusion-sustaining explanation: Peter, who was felt by the reader a moment ago to be near the breaking point ("I don't care what you call it...") is now forced back into the position of a collaborator in self-deception. Their friend "had to pretend to admit, when pressed by Mrs. Mallow, that those aesthetic vices had been the objects of his dread." Peter knows that Lance, like his father, is no good, but ends by participating in the pretense that the great talents of the Mallows might again transcend recognition.

At this point in the story we jump forward in time one year, and Lance, returning from Paris, claims enlightenment, and in so doing serves as the harbinger of an as yet unknown, deeper, and disturbing truth. "I know now why you were so much against it... Something rather awful has happened to me. It *isn't* so very good to know." The ever-cautious Peter, however, wary of knowledge to the extent that this wariness itself, as we shall see, requires explanation, sounds out Lance before giving the known thing a name. Although Peter can see that Lance has changed, or, more precisely, has been altered by what he knows ("something of his bloom seemed really to have left him"), Peter nevertheless asks, "Still, are you very sure you do know?" Lance's answer, inside the text, is insufficient for Peter to identify the feared truth. Beyond the text it shows that knowledge is on occasion the sort of thing that can only be handled in certain quantities. He replies, "Well, I at least know about as much as I can bear." This epistemological chess game between the two continues, with Peter asking whether Lance knows what "in particular" he was afraid of, and Lance answering that "in particular there can only have been one thing," which is that he is *himself* a "beastly duffer," that is, wholly without talent. Of course Peter turns away, as James carefully tells us, "almost with relief." James is, through this carefully guarded conversation, showing that knowledge possesses yet another peculiar characteristic; it is the sort of thing we can circumnavigate, with the most extreme caution, without directly or explicitly acknowledging. The conversation is, in Lance's mind, about his own newly acquired awareness of his own limitations and how his experience in Paris verified the "deep doubt of his means." In Peter's mind the interest of the conversation lies not in what it is about, but in what it is *not* about; it is narrowly averting the fearful subject, not of Lance's but of the Master's shortcomings. Hidden knowledge, however, is easily sensed: because of Peter's incompletely suppressed sense of relief at the fact that Lance does not know after all about his father's artistic shortcomings, and the total absence of recrimination, Lance is driven to ask Peter a few days later what it was *precisely* that Peter was afraid he should find out through his experience in Paris. Peter refused "on the ground that if he hadn't yet guessed perhaps he never would... and that in any case nothing at all for either of them was to be gained by giving the thing a name." The epistemological lesson of this last line is obvious; knowledge of this sensed-but-circumnavigated variety, once named, can take on a force it otherwise cannot exhibit. But Lance, because of this remark of Peter's, is left in suspense, which he later expresses: "Do you know your conundrum has been keeping me awake?" In their next meeting it is clear to Peter upon one glance that Lance has in fact understood, and moreover Peter can see that Lance is only waiting for a moment alone with him to flaunt his new revelation. What James reveals about knowledge in this episode is that the condition of knowing, in the right circumstances, is something that is, to the right person, plainly visible from the outside. Peter, with one look at Lance even in what is in this case the supremely repressive company of the Mallows, sees instantly that Lance now knows that the words "The Master," rather than embodying the truth, only hold the truth at bay.

Lance later informs Peter that he understood the "true value" of the Master's work as soon as he began to understand anything, but that it was not until he got to Paris that he began *fully* to know. This piece of literary fiction translates rather quickly into philosophical fact; knowing is not something that, at least in cases such as this, is either "on" or "off." The relationships we may have to the truth, as Lance's remarks here show, cannot be captured simply; there are countless intermediate points between ignorance and knowledge. But there is here a deeper lesson concerning knowledge embedded in the text as well. Lance, seizing his chance, exclaims to Peter,

"I'm a hopeless muff—that I *had* to have rubbed in. But I'm not such a muff as the Master!" From this vantage point one can observe the "organic" connections between seemingly isolated articles of knowledge. In learning about himself Lance also learns the truth about his father. To condense this passage into a philosophical assertion, we might say that revelations are interdependent in a way that eludes any simple propositional definition of truth.[12]

Another strand of this rather tangled web is explored next. Lance quite understandably now wants to know how Peter has, for all these years, "managed to keep bottled." And with a combination of gravity and embarrassment, showing that the conversation is now swerving out of control and is headed straight for Peter's darkest secret, Peter, hinting at a confession, replies, "It was for your mother." Underscoring the fearfulness of this fact, he demands from Lance a solemn vow to "sacrifice anything rather than let her ever guess" that the Master's work is of no value and that both Peter and Lance know it. After, however, a few more trips between Carrera Lodge and Paris, which only heighten the contrast in Lance's mind between artistic success and failure, and following a few conversations with his father in which the Master places heavy demands of artistic productivity on his son, the tension between appearance and

12. Perhaps the greatest elucidation of this propositional conception of truth is to be found in Wittgenstein's own early work; see his *Tractatus Logico-Philosophicus*, trans. D. F. Pears and B. F. McGuinness (London: Routledge & Kegan Paul, 1961). Moreover, although this point is not made within the context of James's story, the understanding, or the extent to which one knows the truth of any given proposition, is not an all-or-nothing affair. In short, the propositional conception of truth is further challenged by the fact that the same string of words can hold very different—and independently correct—meanings to different users. For a discussion of this point in its theological setting, see Renford Bambrough, *Reason, Truth, and God* (London: Methuen, 1969), esp. chapter 2, "Olympus." It might also be said here, against the propositional conception, that in aesthetics and critical contexts it becomes plain that to utter a true (but isolated) statement about a work is very far from providing an accurate characterization of it.

reality, now of course urgently felt by Lance as well as Peter, mounts. Lance's knowledge thus becomes a burden "heavier ... than ... flesh and blood could bear," and Lance warns Peter than an explosion is imminent. Along the course toward this end we see how shared knowledge can pull people together ("The closest if not quite the gayest relation they [Peter and Lance] had yet known together was thus ushered in"), how imbalances of knowledge can add "between the parties a shade of alienation," and how certain varieties of self-knowledge can induce paralysis ("even if the lesson [of returning to Paris] were simply that of one's impotence in the presence of one's larger vision"). We learn as well—and we shall consider the effects of this revelation on Peter below—that Mrs. Mallow *does* know the truth about her husband's work, and that she too has silently carried, hidden from others, this knowledge, which radically and suddenly transforms our understanding of her as a person. This act of prolonged protective concealment is taken by Lance as proof of how "tremendously much" she does care for her husband. For Peter the question of the morality of participation in deception is not so clear; the next line of the text is "Wonderful, Peter mused." He obviously does not share Lance's enthusiasm. The philosophical lesson we here learn from literature is that knowledge itself is not, as traditional and dubious distinctions between facts and values would imply, morally inert.[13]

We must now turn to further and deeper questions concerning Peter, which will lead us to the final rather mystifying category of knowledge. This peculiar variety might arguably be classified as a species of self-deception of the Morgan-genus, that is, one of the things we ought to know but do not, but it

---

13. I refer here to the variety of distinctions drawn between facts and values, by, for example, G. E. Moore, H. A. Prichard, positivists, and emotivists, and as disputed by those in the pragmatic tradition, such as Charles Peirce.

is in fact the subtle differences rather than the larger similarities with self-deception that are of greater interest.

Let us consider a small collection of Peter's words and deeds from the story. He has, from the beginning of the story, occupied the position of relative enlightenment. But it is only relative, as there are things about himself that, at the end of the story, he realizes are true and that had in fact motivated him all along. And yet, unlike the Master, it cannot be said of him that he was clearly in a state of self-deception. It is true, however, that he possesses a history, developed as the story progresses, of avoidance.[14] When he demands from Lance his promise to sacrifice anything rather than let his mother guess the truth, Lance says, "But what is it you've in mind that I may have a chance to sacrifice" to which Peter replies, "Oh one always has something." Lance, with only partial comprehension, asks, "Do you mean that *you've* had—?" but our narrator informs us that "the look he received back ... so put the question by that he soon enough found another." This is, for Peter, a brush with the too-true, so much so that James has Peter reply, not with words, which might in some oblique way acknowledge, or even give a name to, the dark fact of his long-standing love for Lance's mother, but rather with a forbidding look, stern enough to stop Lance in mid-sentence. Peter next explains to Lance that the keeping of the secret of the Master's failings is so crucial because the Master's "little public" is so tiny, where "any individual dropping out [will be] too dreadfully missed." The epistemological significance of this explanation is that it is simultaneously true

14. Of course, from a pragmatic epistemology, the fact that knowledge itself can function in this instrumental or causal way would not be surprising, since on that view inquiry is conducted by *inquirers* who are engaged with whatever epistemological issue is at hand; this stands in direct opposition to the more traditional philosophical view in which abstract detachment is regarded as prerequisite for epistemological inquiry.

and false. On one level, it is indeed true that any loss of Morgan's public—the slightly extended family—would be tremendously damaging to their private myth of artistic preeminence. But on another level, of which Peter is still at this point explicitly unaware and only dimly senses, it is a mere rationalization; he wants to get Lance safely bottled up without admitting that an exposure would force him to face a number of very serious questions in his life which he would prefer to comfortably avoid. A troubled status quo is, for Peter, preferable to an inward revolution.

The text offers much further evidence of these deeper-level machinations in which obstacles are carefully placed between the self and the truth. Lance later asks Peter, "and what do you regard in particular...as the danger?" Peter answers, "Why this certainly: that the moment your mother, who feels so strongly, should suspect your secret—well...the fat would be on the fire." The textual evidence of special interest here lies again, not in what is present, but in what is absent. Peter avoids a specific answer by putting in its place, and after a moment of desperate conversational searching signaled in the text by the ellipsis, a cliché. Nevertheless, in spite of himself and his obvious desire to truncate extremely his participation in this dialogue, he does approximate an answer. Lance, worried about what would happen if his mother did learn the truth from her son about her husband, asks, "She'd throw me over?" and Peter answers abruptly, "She'd throw *him* [Morgan] over." This eventuality would of course bring to Peter's world a chaos and urgency that, because of his hidden love for Mrs. Mallow, would prove to be too much to bear.

This tactic of retreating behind a cliché to avoid answering a question occurs more than once in the story. When Lance is on the verge of exposing everything, he asks Peter how after all this time he has been able to "keep the game up," to pretend that Morgan is in fact a master. He answers "...I have my reason," and, after Lance determines that the reason is no other

Interpretation and Philosophical Method 167

than his own mother, Peter says, "What will you have? I haven't ceased to like her." Lance here presses further by asking, "But what is she to you, after all, and what is it to you that, as to anything whatever, she should or she shouldn't?" In response to this strong invitation to face the truth squarely, Peter again evades giving a meaningful answer: "Well, it's all simply what I make of it." But Lance now exhibits "a strange, an adopted insistence," strange because it is clearly intrusive, and adopted because its intrusive stance is alien to Lance's character and to his normal acknowledgement of Peter's right to privacy, and, peering into sensed but still unknown dimensions of Peter's inner life, presses further. James is here revealing another curious characteristic of a certain variety of knowledge, specifically that we can sense the presence of some fact and pursue it, without, in a fashion that initially appears self-contradictory, knowing it. We can feel its presence and know that it is operative without knowing what it is. Finally, Lance almost spells it out, saying, "How awfully—always—you must have like her!" and Peter, in a way that is revealing but, because of its brevity, simultaneously concealing, confesses: "Awfully. Always." One can see here that Peter has found the maintenance of the illusion to be one way, an odd way, of protecting the object of his love. We see here that, as in the case of Mrs. Mallow, the maintenance of imbalances of knowledge can hold not only epistemological but emotional significance. Here too facts and feelings are not unrelated in the way theories of knowledge might lead us to expect.

The self-realization Peter reaches is far deeper. At the close of the story Lance, having learned the very striking fact that his mother *has* always known, and having revealed this to Peter, remarks on the futility of Peter's attempt to keep Lance from Paris and thus Mrs. Mallow from the truth about her husband. Lost in a self-absorbed gaze, Peter, in the final line of the story, answers Lance from his own unguarded self, "I think it must have been—without my quite at the time knowing it—to keep *me!*" This claim—that it must have all along been in truth a scheme to keep himself from knowledge and its attendant problems—is the single example in the story of the last and most problematic variety of knowledge. Here, in retrospect, one can see that it did motivate Peter all along, and yet all the other concerns visible on the surface, such as protecting his friend Morgan from a sense of failure, protecting Mrs. Mallow from the sad truth about Morgan's failure, and protecting Lance from disillusionment with his father, were not insincere or *merely* inauthentic layers of rationalization. But Peter does not see the veiled truth: he was, in the final analysis, protecting himself. How, precisely, has Peter done this? What does Peter now see, something not explicitly given in the story, of which he was afraid all along?

Peter, as we have seen, has lost his somewhat strange protective attitude toward Mrs. Mallow, that is, his very personal means of expressing his love for her. And it may also be that, in one part of his mind, he too, with Lance, thinks that she is "too wonderful" in quietly sustaining what she also knows to be illusion. But these are not the most difficult problems arising from Peter's reluctant achievement of self-knowledge. Now that Peter knows that Mrs. Mallow knows the truth about her husband's life work, she is, even if the generously kind Peter would not want to recognize this rather cruel fact, available to him in a way she previously was not. She might, given the right condition, indeed be induced to "throw him [Morgan] over." Moreover, learning of this utterly unsuspected knowledge in Mrs. Mallow's possession would surely lead Peter to ask himself what *else* she secretly knows, particularly about his own inner emotional life, which he always assumed to be invisible to the external world. Indeed, it is now possible that when Mrs. Mallow told Peter he knew nothing of passion she was saying one thing and thinking quite the opposite. In short, Peter must now ask himself, with considerable urgency, what he ought to do and what must be done now that things are known to be as they really are. Given that the positions of the characters have drastically changed with respect to knowledge, Peter must act. James shows us here, most vividly, that what might initially appear as intangible an entity as knowledge can operate in the world as a powerful causal agent.[15] Here, however, the story ends; we do not as readers see the influence knowledge has on action. Indeed, one dimension of this story's quality, and of its mimetic fidelity, derives from the fact that this intensely serious question is left, for Peter, painfully open.

Literary Interpretation and Philosophical Investigation

Let us return from literature to philosophy. In answer to the question "What is knowledge?" we might now answer with conviction, against the presumption that the unitary answer implicitly demanded by the question is possible, that knowledge appears in a number of varieties and that it exhibits a fairly diverse set of characteristics. To summarize, we have found, in the first section: (1) things we know and which are plain and obvious to others; (2) things we know of ourselves but which remain hidden from others, such as Peter's love for Mrs. Mallow; (3) things others do know, or can know, about us which we do not, and which we, in present circumstances or without further evidence, cannot know, such as Lance's ignorance concerning his own abilities as an artist before he travels to Paris; (4) things others know about us which we presently do not, but which we could, and in some cases should, know, such as the Master's self-knowledge or lack thereof; and (5) things we know but, as epistemological burdens, regret having come to know,

15. For a discussion of this characteristic, see Renford Bambrough, "Thought, Word, and Deed," *Proceedings of the Aristotelian Society*, supp. vol. (1980): 105–17.

such as Peter's foreknowledge of Lance's artistic failure. In the second section we saw many of the diverse characteristics of knowledge: (1) knowledge can be something of which we can be warned and that we are in some contexts better off not knowing; (2) happiness can be a function of knowledge; (3) the nature and quality of relationships can be determined by what the members of those relationships know; (4) the act of self-deception or the avoidance of knowledge can be extremely intricate, and spurious knowledge demonstrates remarkable resilience in the face of facts; (5) knowledge is the sort of thing with which one can behave subtly or crudely, and it can sometimes be tolerable only in fragments; (6) knowledge can be cautiously and delicately avoided,[16] in both word and deed, without—apparently paradoxically—recognizing its existence; (7) a mere glimmer of understanding can be, through the simple act of naming it and thereby rendering it explicit, curiously empowered, as the very act of replacing substance with euphemism often acknowledges; (8) knowledge is, in some contexts and to some viewers, impossible to conceal; (9) separate articles of knowledge intertwine in complex ways, so that to know one thing is often to have satisfied a precondition for knowing another; (10) knowledge itself possesses the power to determine the emotional climate; for example facts alone can induce feelings of closeness, alienation, confidence, futility, or urgency; (11) our conception of a person's character is in a sense "sculpted" over time by the knowledge we possess of that person; (12) explanations of our own actions, or self-knowledge, can, in a paradoxical way, be simultaneously false (when approaching rationalization) and true (when approaching revelation); (13) the preservation of an imbalance of knowledge can itself be an emotionally expressive gesture; (14)

---

16. I borrow this term from Stanley Cavell, "The Avoidance of Love: A Reading of King Lear," in *Must We Mean What We Say?* (New York: Charles Scribner's Sons, 1969).

knowledge can, while remaining hidden, guide our behavior toward certain ends unwittingly; and (15) knowledge can, with a strength as great as any immediate physical cause, force us to act.

Of course, the context-specific lists of the varieties of knowledge found in this story can, but ought not to be, confused with the establishment of rigid and exhaustive epistemological categories. It is true that this particular manifestation of the impulse to philosophical essentialism would not be unitary (in that there are many categories rather than only one), but it would still certainly be foreign to both the Wittgensteinian and the Jamesian projects as investigated in all of the foregoing. In fact, one should employ all such lists in the provisional and context-specific ways one arrives at them, remembering that they are categories whose content, applicability, and their very definition depend on a specific context. And they are no more mutually exclusive than they are rigid; an article of hidden knowledge may force us to act in preserving an imbalance of knowledge, or the knowledge that we are deliberately replacing descriptive substance with euphemism in order to preserve a conception of a person's character may be impossible to conceal. Such lists should be employed, then, as reminders of ground covered, as means to improve and clarify the understanding of problematic concepts.

The end of philosophy, in Wittgenstein's later view, is not the construction or elaboration of theories but rather the attainment of a kind of overview (*Übersicht*) of philosophically problematic concepts and their complex interrelations.[17] This overview itself is the result of an investigation into particular sectors of actual linguistic practice. Although valuable for quite a number of reasons, such an overview is primarily intended

---

17. See the clear discussion of this concept in G. P. Baker and P.M.S. Hacker, *Wittgenstein: Understanding and Meaning* (Chicago: University of Chicago Press, 1980), pp. 531–45.

to effect not a solution but a dissolution of philosophical puzzlement. And puzzlement, which for us takes form in the question "What is knowledge?" is, when diagnosed one way, itself the result of jumping to unwarranted conclusions from the surface appearance of language; for as the word "knowledge" is used in all the varieties and with all the characteristics we have considered, the conclusion is that there must be an essence present in all those cases. To preserve the illusion of epistemological essence, when doing philosophy we select only those cases that conform to our conceptual expectations, leaving any recalcitrant cases out of consideration. This unwitting methodological habit, which itself nourishes the sense of philosophical puzzlement, Wittgenstein referred to as a "one-sided diet" of examples.[18] We are, in fact, now in position to see that traditional or foundationalist epistemology exhibits this propensity. The questions asked of knowledge are largely contained in the first variety, for example, how do we *know* a table exists?[19] And G. E. Moore's famous defense of common sense, developed against this kind of question, is contained within this category.[20]

One might with some accuracy say that the later Wittgenstein was far more concerned with philosophical *questions*, and their resident presumptions, than with answers. The accuracy of this remark is, however, only partial; this way of putting the matter implies that answers are still the ultimate goal, but that some preparatory work—analyzing and clarifying the question—

---

18. See Ludwig Wittgenstein, *Philosophical Investigations*, 3d ed., trans. G. E. M. Anscombe (New York: Macmillan, 1953), sec. 593. It might be noted again here that even at the source of this philosophical method in the Platonic dialogues Socrates is himself better in practice than his theory would suggest, since he very frequently finds argumentative progression through the employment of counterexamples.

19. This is of course the very question Bertrand Russell addresses in *The Problems of Philosophy* (Oxford: Oxford University Press, 1912), pp. 7–16.

20. G. E. Moore, "A Defense of Common Sense," in *Philosophical Papers* (London: Allen & Unwin, 1959).

must be done first. But the acquisition of a conceptual overview, itself the result of judiciously and patiently assembling cases of both actual and imaginary linguistic practice within specified contexts of the sort discussed in Chapters 3 and 4, is not merely a way of preparing for philosophical activity, it *is* philosophical activity.

We might very roughly characterize the methods of science as assembling data and explaining it as fully as possible within a comprehensive and unified theory, which itself progresses as new data demand inclusion.[21] According to Wittgenstein, this kind of methodological progression is foreign to the mission of philosophy and, providing it wants to avoid complicated entanglements in conceptual confusion, it ought not to try in this way to emulate science. For Wittgenstein, philosophy does not, *in this sense*, progress.[22] But it would be deeply erroneous to infer, as many have done, that Wittgenstein thus concluded that philosophy does not in any sense progress. The notion of philosophy leaving everything as it is can indeed very easily be misunderstood. Philosophy, although it may leave the world alone,[23] certainly does not leave our *thought* about that world alone. Again, the attainment of an overview is itself an achievement, a sign of progress of a distinctively philosophical sort which will free us from the particular puzzlement that motivated the initial philosophical questions. This progress has, in fact, been likened to psychoanalysis, through its concern with the excavation and explanation of deeply embedded presump-

---

21. Regardless of the accuracy or legitimacy of this characterization of science it is certainly the conception Wittgenstein had in mind when he warned of a "preoccupation with the methods of science," in *The Blue and Brown Books* (Oxford: Basil Blackwell, 1958), pp. 18–20. This characterization does not recognize the variety of science, and as such, while offered by Wittgenstein in this transitional work, is not "Wittgensteinian."

22. See *Philosophical Investigations*, sec. 126.

23. I owe this particular way of putting the matter, with its metaphilosophical resonance, to Jonathan Lear, "On Leaving the World Alone," *Journal of Philosophy* 79 (July 1982): 382–403.

tions or beliefs that, beneath the level of conscious deliberation, influence thought and behavior.[24]

In a well-known passage in his *Confessions*, Augustine provides a perfect microcosm of Wittgenstein's methodology. Augustine puzzles over the nature of time, and he observes that although in the course of daily life he knows, indeed he *must* know, what time is, when asked directly he finds himself quite perplexed. Wittgenstein says of Augustine's problem, "Something that we know when no one asks us, but no longer know when we are supposed to give an account of it, is something that we need to *remind* ourselves of. (And it is obviously something of which for some reason it is difficult to remind oneself.)"[25] Our difficulty, of course, is that achieving an overview is impossible while holding to the essentialist presumption concerning the common element and while failing to perceive the great diversity present within the concept of knowledge; that is, while holding to a one-sided diet of examples. Thus in this way too we arrive at the central method of philosophical therapy, that of assembling reminders of how we actually use philosophically problematic words and how we actually investigate the distinctions and contrasts those words make in particular contexts.[26] This also provides at least some insight into the meaning of Wittgenstein's famous dictum, "Ask not for the meaning, but for the use."[27] To inquire, with Augustine, into the nature of time "out of context" or in isolation from this word's contextually determined counterparts, is to allow language to "go on holiday,"[28] that is, to separate a word from the

---

24. See Wisdom, *Philosophy and Psycho-analysis*, pp. 169–81.
25. *Philosophical Investigations*, sec. 89. For an insightful employment of this technique in connection with literature see D. Z. Phillips, *Through a Darkening Glass: Philosophy, Literature, and Cultural Change* (Notre Dame, Ind.: University of Notre Dame Press, 1982).
26. See *Philosophical Investigations*, secs. 127, and then 89 and 253.
27. See *Philosophical Investigations*, secs. 43, and then 30, 138, 120, and 179.
28. See *Philosophical Investigations*, sec. 38.

very context that ensures its intelligibility. We then further assume that the word, quite apart from that context, functions as a name through its inviolable signification of, if not a person or object, then a property, attribute, or quality. This further assumption, that words which occupy positions near the center of philosophy—knowledge, truth, value, meaning, justice, reality, and so on—function as names brings us to one last aspect of Wittgenstein's later methodology. Like Nietzsche before him, who conceived of language as a "cemetery of metaphors"[29] and as a conceptual prison, Wittgenstein believed that language, if not a cemetery of metaphors then certainly a repository of illusion, possesses the power to "bewitch our intelligence"[30] and to lead us to face questions that, having assumed the appearance of great metaphysical profundity, are in the final analysis incoherent;[31] that is, they are not only words but questions detached from their necessary contextual conditions for intelligibility. The power of language to bewitch derives from a "picture" (*Urbild*) which is embedded in our language but of which we, as speaker-victims, are utterly unaware; here too the analogy with psychoanalysis is apt. The operative "picture" in this case, resting beneath the presumption concerning the naming-function of central philosophical words, is that words function as labels and acquire meaning through reaching out to particulars in the world to which they directly refer.[32] This is,

29. For a discussion of this dimension of Nietzsche's philosophy of language and its connection to aesthetic theory, see Arthur Danto, "Art and Irrationality," in *Nietzsche as Philosopher* (New York: Columbia University Press, 1980).

30. For a diagnosis of recent aesthetic theories concerning the ontology of art as manifestations of bewitched intelligence, see B. R. Tilghman, *But Is It Art?* (Oxford: Basil Blackwell, 1984), esp. "Afterword," pp. 187–89.

31. This is the sense in which there is a direct continuity between the early Wittgenstein of the *Tractatus* and the later; both are concerned with the delineation (to appropriate a Kantian-Strawsonian title) of the bounds of sense.

32. The results of applying this model of reference to aesthetic theory are discussed in my "Art and the Unsayable: Langer's Tractarian Aesthetics," *British Journal of Aesthetics* 24 (Autumn 1984): 325–40.

of course, the issue with which Wittgenstein initiated *Philosophical Investigations*, this view having resided implicitly in Russell's work in the philosophy of language[33] and which also provided the center of gravity in *Tractatus Logico-Philosophicus*. And although the question of linguistic reference would take us back again into the issues discussed in Chapters 1 and 2,[34] it does at this juncture provide one illustration of how a picture, in this case of meaning and the specific way in which words refer to the world, determines how a philosophical question is formed and what sort of answer one thus expects to it.[35]

Of course, this larger methodological analogy with psychoanalysis should be applied to the fundamental problems not just in this chapter, but to all of the foregoing. The overly general and conceptually presumptuous formulations of (1) questions that trouble us about the nature of linguistic meaning and its relation to artistic meaning, (2) questions unwittingly and misleadingly housing extensionalism inside the parallel problems of person-perception and artwork-perception, and (3) questions leading us to attempt to satisfy a craving for a unitary encapsulation of literary meaning are all questions to be particularized, to be worked through, and—ultimately—abandoned.[36] They are questions about which we can achieve,

---

33. Bertrand Russell, *Inquiries into Meaning and Truth* (Harmondsworth: Penguin, 1965).

34. See *Philosophical Investigations*, secs. 109, 116, 156–64, and *The Blue and Brown Books*, p. 18.

35. For a thorough development of this dimension of Wittgenstein's philosophy, see F. B. Ebersole, *Things We Know* (Eugene: University of Oregon Press, 1967). Also, for uniquely sustained attention to linguistic detail and its significance for the dissolution of philosophical problems, see his *Language and Perception* (Washington, D.C.: University Press of America, 1979) and *Meaning and Saying* (Washington, D.C.: University Press of America, 1979).

36. See, for example, the accurate diagnoses as well as the extremely positive therapeutic results following the disentangling of questions of literary meaning from those of psychological and epistemic privileged access, in Laurent Stern, " 'Words Fail Me,' " *Journal of Aesthetics and Art Criticism* 43 (Fall 1984): 57–69; consider also in the present context his translation of a

to a greater or lesser extent and after the conceptual therapy of philosophical investigation, a certain peace. Indeed, it is through the descent to particularity that we are enabled to answer those larger haunting questions properly; the way *not* to answer them is to accept their conceptual prescriptions and explanatory expectations and give them answers on the level of generality at which they are asked.

To our question at the core of this final chapter, "What is Knowledge?" we would answer, under the influence of the picture of meaning sketched just above, that is, word-to-world reference, that knowledge is what we are in possession of only where the sentence we form to express a proposition, or knowledge-claim, corresponds directly to what is in fact the case in the world, and when we have, through empirical observation, verified that correspondence. But this answer, from the vantage point or, indeed, the overview we have achieved through the interpretation of James's story, now appears hopelessly reductive, simplistic, and, most important, and like much else in philosophy that proceeds in a positivistic style, far less than authentically illuminating. To assemble one final list, we have seen among Wittgensteinian techniques: (1) a replacement of solution with dissolution; (2) a sensitivity to a one-sided diet of examples; (3) an overall anti-essentialism; (4) a concern for acquiring an overview instead of a theory; (5) an analogy with psychoanalysis; (6) a concern for the use of language and the context justifying that use; (7) an awareness of the power of language to mislead through its implicit "pictures"; (8) a concern with questions rather than answers; and (9) a new conception of philosophical progress.[37] With all of this behind us,

---

passage from Wittgenstein's "Typescript 213": "Human beings are deeply entangled in philosophical, i.e. grammatical confusions. And, to liberate them from these, *requires* that they are torn free from the most multifarious bonds in which they are held captive."

37. This list is intended, of course, only as a sketch. As Baker and Hacker have observed in *Wittgenstein: Understanding and Meaning*, p. 531, it is every bit

the traditional essentialist claims that knowledge is either justified true belief or verified correspondence between proposition and world do indeed appear deeply suspicious. But more important—and here is one sign of philosophical progress of the Wittgensteinian sort—the question to which they are formed as responses is now something we can no longer enthusiastically and unwarily embrace. The questions "What is knowledge?" and "What is the meaning of 'knowledge'?" are perhaps not fundamentally dissimilar. Wittgenstein stated at one point, for reasons that are now perhaps comprehensible, that "only in the stream of thought and life do words have meaning."[38] "Knowledge" is too, after all, a word. And it is not a philosophical theory, but in the present case a work of fiction which presents to us, with great delicacy and sensitivity, the stream of thought and life in which the word, in some of its many varieties and characteristics, is significant. It is in this way that literary interpretation is philosophical investigation.

---

as difficult to attain an overview of an *Übersicht* as it is any other difficult philosophical concept.

38. Ludwig Wittgenstein, *Zettel*, ed. G. E. M. Anscombe and G. H. von Wright, trans. G. E. M. Anscombe (Oxford: Basil Blackwell, 1967), sec. 173.

~ Index

Abstract gestures, 76
Ackermann, Robert John, 24n
Aesthetic and moral description, 117
Aesthetic decline, 106
Aesthetic identity, 117
Aesthetic integrity, 117
Aestheticism, 89, 92, 93
Aesthetic mentalism, 52
Aesthetic patience, 134
Aesthetic realism, 125
Aesthetic relativism, 125
Aldrich, Virgil, 2n
Alpers, Svetlana, 26n
Ambiguity, 114, 115, 116, 118, 126, 128
Aquinas, 74
Archimedean points of meaning, 18
Architectural microcosm, 39
Art:
  evil power of, 93, 102
  and life, inversion of, 103
Art-as-language, 44, 45, 53, 59
Artistic limits, 37, 44
Artistic purity, 35
Artistic transgression, 33–36
Aspectival ambiguity, 104, 128
Aspect perception, 2, 3, 7, 57, 90–91, 109, 111, 119
Aspects of organization, 127
Atomism, linguistic, 7
Attitude, 135, 136, 137
Attitude towards a soul, 133

Auditory language, 36
Augustine's *Confessions*, 13, 174
Authorial integrity, 116
Avoidance, linguistic, 165, 166
Ayer, A. J., 150n

Bach, J. S., 35
Baker, Benjamin, 30
Baker, G. P., 34n, 63n, 171n, 177n
Bambrough, Renford, 7n, 25n, 46n, 149n, 169n
Bartok, Bela, 30, 42
Baxandall, Michael, 30n, 40n, 77, 78, 81
Bayeux tapestry, 26
Bedrock, 67
Behavior, shades of, 127
Berg, Alban, 37
Borges, Jorge Luis, 66n
Borromini, Francesco, 130n
Botticelli, Sandro, 78
Boulez, Pierre, 37
Bounds of description, 102
Bronzino, 75
Bryson, Norman, 18n
Builders, 13, 19, 20, 35, 36, 38, 84, 86
Byzantine influence, 39

Cage, John, 27
Cantos, 74
Carroll, Lewis, 17
Carter, Elliott, 71

Casey, John, 2n
Cavell, Stanley, 170n
Cave paintings, 69
Certainty, 48, 50, 55, 82, 133, 135
Cezanne, Paul, 36
Cioffi, Frank, 3n, 56n
Circumstances of meaning, 86
Classical orders, 34, 66
Close reading, 123, 134
Cohen, Ted, 2n
Combinatorial reach, 38
"Common behavior of mankind," 51, 75
Complicating relations, 103
Compositional determinism, 38–39
Compositional possibilities, 41
Compositional ratiocination, 64
Conceptual overview, 173, 174
Conceptual peace, 177
Conceptual prison, 175
Consciousness, shades of, 76
Critical encapsulation, 141, 142, 144
Critical justification, 4–5
Critical puzzle, 139

Dali, Salvador, 81
Dante Alighieri, 31, 74, 75
Danto, Arthur, 65n, 29n
David, Jacques-Louis, 26, 80
Dawning of an aspect, 58, 118, 125, 129
Debussy, Claude, 31, 36, 66
Definition, 2, 3
Degas, Edgar, 112n
de Kooning, Willem, 35
Depth grammar, 59, 60
Descriptions of persons and of artifacts, 86
Design-vocabulary, 34
Dickie, George, 2n, 133n, 138n
Dissolution, 172
Dualistic mentalism, 59
Dualistic metaphysics, 131
Duchampian question, 130
Dürer, Albrecht, 26, 94

Ebersole, F. B., 65n, 176n
Eldridge, Richard, 2n
El Greco, 30n
Elliott, R. K., 3n

Emergent properties, 131
Emotion, concept of, 69
Emotive-descriptive terms, 4, 5
Encapsulation, 176
English portraiture, 28
Epistemological "buried treasure," 143
Essence, essentialism, 25n, 32, 53, 54, 76, 135, 149, 150, 171, 172, 177, 178
Ethical and aesthetic descriptions, 86
Ethical and aesthetic perception, 66
Ethical and aesthetic reasoning, 126
Evidence, 109, 112, 113, 115
Explanation beyond description, 68
Explanatory generality, 4
Extensionalism, 4, 107

Face-as-text, 110
Facial expressivity, 7, 67, 69, 87, 106, 133
Facial gestures, 78
Facial interpretation, 125
Facial resemblance, 56
Family resemblance, 2
Fictional web, 87
Fingarette, Herbert, 155n
"Five-red-apples," 11, 13
Following a rule, 51, 62, 63, 64, 67
Form of life, 5, 23, 45–59, 59–69, 95, 104, 133, 136, 138
  agreement in, 47, 80
Fra Roberto, 77, 78
Frazer, Sir James George, 50–59
Frege, Gottlob, 40
Fugue, 30

Gauguin, Paul, 27, 58n
Genius loci, 90
Gershwin, George, 35
Gesture, 50–55, 78, 79, 80, 117, 120, 127, 142, 165
  gestural expression, 7, 95, 97, 98, 102
  gestural meaning, 99
  gestural power of language, 54
Gettier, E. L., 150n
Gilmour, John, 27n
Giotto, 81
Given, the, 50, 58, 59, 66
Goehr, Alexander, 70n

Index 181

Goya y Lucientes, Francisco José de, 29
Graves, Michael, 43
Guston, Philip, 39

Hacker, P. M. S., 34n, 63n, 171n, 177n
Hallett, Garth, 150–151n
Haydn, Franz Joseph, 64
Hogarth, William, 28
Hunter, J. F. M., 18n, 23n

Imaginative seeing, 2, 89
Impatience, 134
Impressionist movement, 27
Incompatible descriptions, 87
Ineffable, 20, 46, 99
Internal relation, 58
Interpretation:
　ambiguity and, 121
　epistemology and, 124
　objectivity and, 126n
　relativism and, 122, 124
　skepticism and, 143
　vision and, 140
Introspection, 68
Investigation, 149, 150, 151, 177
Irreducibility, 7
Ives, Charles, 31

James, William, 112n
Jazz improvisation, 72
Johnson, Philip, 39
Justified true belief, 150

Keifer, Anselm, 39
Kermode, Frank, 84n, 85, 86, 93, 105n, 121n, 147n
Knowledge:
　categories of, 152–55, 164
　characteristics of, 170, 171
　See also Self-knowledge
Korsmeyer, Carolyn, 2n
Kripke, Saul, 63n

Language:
　essence of, 13
　foundations of, 55n
　limits of, 17, 20, 36, 44
　mastery of, 21–22
　primitive forms of, 9, 11, 45
　use of, 15, 17
　visual, 43
　See also Linguistic *entries*
Language-as-city, 24, 32–33
Language-game, 5, 9–17, 17–24, 24–44, 93, 114, 116, 121, 129, 132
　expansion and growth of, 15, 23–24, 34, 89–91
　locutionary possibilities, 21
　nonverbal, 50
　permutations, 21
　possible misunderstandings, 15, 16
　self-sufficiency, 18, 18n, 21
　transgression of, 22, 41, 49
Lear, Jonathan, 65n, 173n
Leavis, F. R., 147n
Leonardo da Vinci, 26
Lerner, Laurence, 23n
Levinson, Jerrold, 136
Lewis, P. B., 3n
Lichtenstein, Roy, 73, 74
Linguistic aim and function, 12
Linguistic appearance, superficial, 17
Linguistic community, 46
Linguistic mentalism, 21
Linguistic microcosm, 10, 13, 19, 20
Linguistic possibility, possibilities, 34, 41, 51, 85
Linguistic relativity, 18
Linguistic spirit, 56
Logically primitive agreements in judgment, 64–65n
Lüdeking, Karlheinz, 3n
Lyas, Colin, 110n

Magical realism, 66
Malcolm, Norman, 52, 54n
Mandelbaum, Maurice, 2n
Margolis, Joseph, 65n
Masaccio, 80
Mastery, 39, 40, 42, 45, 49, 62, 67, 81
Meaning:
　separable from saying, 19
　severed from intention, 111
　shades of, 110, 118, 127
Meanings as native residents of contexts, 20
Memento mori, 80
Mental image, 109
Mentalism, 21, 52, 64
Mentalistic conception of meaning, 19

Microcosms, 39, 84
Mimesis, 7, 70, 86, 90, 93, 106, 147, 147n, 148n, 169
Modigliani, Amedeo, 36
Mondrian, Piet, 76
Monet, Claude, 25
Moore, G. E., 164n, 172, 172n
Moral force, 88
Moral proximity through language, 101
Moral sense school, 82n
Moral sensitivity, 88
Mothersill, Mary, 30n
Mozart, Wolfgang Amadeus, 64
Musical minimalism, 41
Mussorgsky, Modest, 30

Natural emotive behavior, 56
Natural expressivity, 78
Newell, R. W., 65n
Nietzsche, Friedrich, 175, 175n

Obeying a rule blindly, 65
O'Neill, Onora, 65n, 69n
Oscillation of aspects, 103, 118, 129
Ostensive definition, 13, 14, 15, 33

Pain, meaning of, 61
Palmer, Anthony, 65n, 132n
Parker, Charlie, 39n, 43
Paterian aestheticism, 87
Patience, 148
Patterns of description, 90, 91
Peirce, Charles, 164n
Perception of persons and of works of art, 86, 131, 138, 148, 176
Perceptual shift, 129
Phillips, D. Z., 174n
Philosophical progress, 3, 173–78
Physicalistic description, 58
Physiognomic properties, 69, 86
Picasso, Pablo, 42, 58n, 112n
Plato, 150n
Pollock, Jackson, 27, 72, 73
Positivistic art history, 57
Positivistic mythology, 123
Postmodernism, 72, 81
Poussin, Nicolas, 28, 29
Prichard, H. A., 164n

Propositional encapsulation, 81, 96, 109, 145, 151
Proust, Marcel, 28
Psychoanalysis, 175
Psychological realism, 100
Public character of meaning, 62

Raphael, 79
Ratiocination, 55–56, 63, 65n, 67
Ratiocinative reconstruction, 138
Rationalization, 168
Rauschenberg, Robert, 35, 74, 75, 76
Reductive encapsulation, 136
Referential meaning, 16, 18, 123
Rembrandt van Rijn, 76
Rhees, Rush, 3n, 50n, 51n, 52, 53, 55n, 56, 57, 58, 81n
Rilke, Rainer Maria, 31, 31n
Ritual, 5, 45, 53
Rockwell, Norman, 42
Rodin, Auguste, 34
Romano, Giulio, 30
Rothko, Mark, 29, 58
Rule-following, 10–12, 23, 24, 39n, 65
Rules of harmony, 66
Russell, Bertrand, 172, 176n

Schönberg, Arnold, 27, 37
Scruton, Roger, 2n, 40n, 130n
Searle, John, 153n
Second Viennese School, 37
Seeing a likeness, 122
Seeing-as, 127
Seeing vs. saying, 145
Self-deception, 8, 157–65, 167, 168
Self-knowledge, 156, 168
Serial composition, 37, 39
Seurat, Georges, 36
Sherman, Cindy, 27
Shiff, Richard, 27n
Shiner, Roger, 2n
Shusterman, Richard, 2n
Sinister aspect, 57
Situated language, 55
Slithy toves, 17
Solipsism, 146
Spirit, 92, 93
  of painting, 79
  of place, 105, 118
  of utterance, 82, 105

Sraffa, Piero, 52
Stern, Laurent, 176n
Stockhausen, Karlheinz, 27
Stolnitz, Jerome, 133n
Stravinsky, Igor, 27, 30, 36, 65, 70
Strawson, P. F., 65n
Style:
   exhaustion of, 42
   expansion of, 41
   limits of, 37
Stylistic language, 35
Surface grammar, 59, 60
Sympathetic imagination, 82n

Tanner, Michael, 82n
Tautologies, 141, 142
Terminal cadence, 64
Text, visual, 75
Theme and variations, 35
Tiepolo, Giovanni Battista, 112n
Tilghman, B. R., 2n, 3n, 149n, 175n
Tone, linguistic, 95–97, 100–101
Traditional harmony, 37
Trajan's column, 26
Transcription as translation, 31
Trilling, Lionel, 123n, 147n

Unmediated expressive significance, 81
Unmediated perception, 4, 67
Unsayable, 20, 38, 41

Use, uses, 21, 44, 60, 61, 62, 72, 84, 95, 123, 171, 174

Van den Toorn, Pieter, 66n
Vanitas, 80
Varieties of knowledge, 151, 167, 169
   of self-knowledge, 164
Varnedoe, Kirk, 23n, 34n, 58n, 112n
Visual commentary, 75
Visual game, 73
Vivaldi, Antonio, 42

Warburg, Aby, 58n
Watson, George, 147n
Webern, Anton von, 37, 39
Web of human relationships, 135, 138
Web of knowledge, 163, 168
Weil, Simone, 137
Weitz, Morris, 2n, 149n
Winch, Peter, 3n, 41n, 47n, 133, 137, 138n
Wisdom, John, 65n, 156n, 174n
Wittgensteinian techniques, 177
Wollheim, Richard, 2n, 3n, 34n, 45n, 50n, 57n, 62n, 111n, 112n
Woodford, Susan, 70n
Words, aim and function of, 11
Word salad, 34
Wright, Frank Lloyd, 30, 43

www.ingramcontent.com/pod-product-compliance
Lightning Source LLC
Chambersburg PA
CBHW031438160426
43195CB00010BB/772